WASH

A BANKS COUNTY TRAGEDY

A Family Story Finally Revealed

LYNN SMITH & GLENN SMITH

TABLE OF CONTENTS

DEDICATED TO...

There are traits in people that may remind a person of a past relative. How many times has somebody commented that he has Grandpa's eyes or his great uncle's nose, or she has Grandma's chin or her aunt's tiny hands? Family DNA gives physical traits familiar to past, present, and future generations. Hair or eye color or maybe face or mouth shape comes from those generations long gone from our memory. Events in the past form the framework of future generations, and the family learns and teaches the formation as the centuries pass. A specific trait is obvious in every member of the family. Family is important and should come first. A person must take care of their family. It is important to make sure it survives.

Dedicating a book to one's family is because they are who we are!

PREFACE

Many adventures begin in the minds of children rambling around dark corners of an old camelback trunk. Hidden deep in the corners of the musty old treasure chest were secrets of vast proportions about things kids should not question. For a child to get in the trunk was a death-defying act. But the curious minds of children pushed that thought aside for another day. Hidden in the trunk were strange relics of years gone by. An old paper umbrella from the orient tucked safely away was someone's souvenir. A pair of old wire-rimmed glasses rested on the tray. On the bottom of the old trunk, a woman's black hat laid with a veil stretched across the front to pull down over the eyes. Women wore black hats at a funeral or church on Sunday.

There were notepads for the farm and lists of the cotton crop sold and livestock bought. Old black and white photos of people not smiling and awkwardly poised stashed away in the trunk's tray protected in plastic. Envelopes of newspaper clippings contained articles about someone who had died, and the names were vague about who they were. Everybody just assumed it was a past relative. Most of the articles had already turned brown from age. A more recent relative clipped the articles from the newspaper and stashed them away to read later about the departed loved one.

Four old newspaper clippings from years and years ago captivated the minds of everyone. Being in the trunk was risky enough as it was, but to ask who the articles were about was a death sentence. It would be almost a century before anyone would go back to piece together those articles and finally learn just who Wash Smith was. After careful research, his story unfolded before our very eyes. A story of youth, love, and adventure came together, and it all started at the bottom of an old musty trunk.

CHAPTER 1:
FINALLY HOME

Ⅰt was an unseasonably hot day for November, and the community was in mourning. As usual, the neighbors stayed up all night with the family when there was a death in the area. The family never left the body alone, and to sit up with the dead was just the way it was in a rural country home. Everyone prepared for a funeral the next day because a lot of work had to be done. When a death happened, the family came together and prepared for the final parting.

They usually held the funeral in the afternoon, so it gave them time to dig the grave. Friends and family gathered at the ultimate resting place with picks and shovels. They worked all morning to open the grave. The people believed it was superstitious to leave a grave open overnight, and they always dug the day of the funeral. Therefore, for reasons of customs, the family dug the grave the day of his funeral.

Today, the funeral is for Wash Smith, a young twenty-year-old, who should have his entire life ahead of him. Everyone who met him liked him, and no one knew if he had any enemies, at least not by the looks of how many attended his funeral. Hundreds of people in and around Mountain View Baptist Church in Banks County came to the burial.

The church had been there for about thirty-three years, and to get to the church, one followed an old, winding red dirt road with ruts equally apart, formed by wagons filled with churchgoers. Around the last curve in the road, the cemetery came into sight. A simple white church appeared nestled in the woods and rested on rocks balanced on top of each other to form the corner posts for the church, which seemed to rest on solid rock.

The building itself was not a spectacular-looking church, but it was the home church for many in attendance. Two front doors lead into where the body would be. The door on the left was for men and the other one for women and children. It was customary for men and women to sit separately for even worship during this time, but also the two doors, along with the many tall windows, helped cool the church during hot days.

People from every section of the county came to pay their last respects to Wash. They walked, rode horses or buggies pulled by horses or oxen, and some rode bicycles to the church. The more affluent families drove cars. It was almost like a holiday or homecoming at the church with so many people attending. People mingled in and around the yard of the old church, talking and whispering about the event of the day and of the days leading up to this day. News had traveled fast about the funeral, so it was hard to tell if they came for the memorial service out of respect to the deceased and his family or if they expected some brawl to burst open or something worse to take place.

Wooden pews lined each side of the aisle that went all the way to the wall. Mourners occupied every seat, and they brought wooden Sunday school chairs that lined the aisle. When the chairs filled, a mourner had to stand. Every inch of the church had someone sitting in a chair or a pew or was standing in any available space. They filled the area for the choir with mourners. Windowsills served as pews for those who were less fortunate and arrived late.

Children sat on the floor or in the laps of a family member. The family opened the windows of the church to help cool down the inside of the warm church and to let those who did not get to the church for one of the coveted seats inside could hear what they could hear from the churchyard. The aisles were full, along with people hanging on the windowsill to see what was going on. They made the wooden floors from pine boards about two inches wide, and the floor would creak with just about every step made. Once everybody was in place, the old church settled down for the solemn moments that were to come.

Many women wore black dresses. Some wore black hats, and some had the veil pulled down over their eyes to cover the tears. The men wore a black tie with a starched white shirt. Everybody in the old country church stood in respect for the family when the procession entered the church. Leading the way into the church was the preacher walking slowly down the aisle. Pallbearers followed, carrying the casket, a simple pine box. The casket rested at the altar of the church, and the pulpit towered behind. As tradition had it, the children carried flowers or plants to place on or around the closed casket. Since flowers were scarce in November, the only flower placed on the casket was a single white wilted rose.

Wash's family was the last to be seated. His mother dressed in black and wore a black hat with the veil pulled down, and she carried a small white handkerchief to catch the tears that flowed so freely down her tired, worn face. She led the family in and went to the pews on the right that she reserved for them earlier. It was a struggle for her to enter, and Wash's brothers helped her down the aisle to her seat. She wanted to be close to his casket. This was not how she had ever imagined her next visit with him would be. She always said it was unnatural for a child to go before a mother. Once the family sat, the church strained to hold those present.

CHAPTER 2:
THE FUNERAL

Sunday, November 23, 1930

During the funeral, mourners sang old hymns that were favorites of the family, "The Old Rugged Cross" and "In the Garden". His family huddled together up front near the casket and tried intently to listen to every word the preacher spoke. The preacher wore his Sunday black suit, a crisp white shirt, and a black-tie and read verses from his well-worn Bible that might ease the family's grief.

After several hymns the family had requested, the preacher slowly stands and reverently walks to the pulpit just behind the casket. At the pulpit, he opens his old Bible to a place that he has marked to start the eulogy for Wash Smith. He says, "Psalm 23 tells us, 'The Lord is my shepherd; I shall not want, and it ends with Yea, though I walk through the valley of the shadow of death, I will fear no evil."

The preacher says, "Most of you know me. I'm Reverend Cecil Murphy, the pastor here at Mountain View. I want to welcome you on behalf of the family as we gather here today to remember Wash Smith."

"Thank you for being here today. Your presence is an affirmation of your love and support for the family of Wash. Although they may not remember every word shared, they will remember your presence for the rest of their lives. Your presence during this solemn occasion shows your love indeed, but do not let it end today. This family is still going to need you in a week, a month, or even a year from now."

"Don't give the family answers to Wash's death. It wouldn't bring Wash back to us and heal the pain in our hearts. Listen to them as they tell stories of Wash. Listen to their hurt, their memories, and their pain. Calmly and patiently, listen. Give them a shoulder to cry on. Sometimes, the best we can do is to help others cry."

"Wash touched all of our lives and each of us feels this loss deeply. We cannot change what has happened. We need to learn from his passing about life, God, and ourselves. When there is so much uncertainty around us, we must turn to what we are certain of. We are certain that Wash loved his family, that Wash loved his friends, and that Wash loved his Savior. God is with us all today, no matter what."

"Today, in our sadness, we can take comfort knowing Wash is with Jesus. That is all that matters in life. We will be together again someday and all the pain and suffering will be no more. Life is not about where you live, what you own, or who you know. God is here with us today. He does not want us to face the pain of losing Wash alone. He will carry us through this valley and will be with you. The Good Book tells us in Revelation 21:4, 'And God shall wipe away all tears from their eyes; and there shall be no more death, neither sorrow, nor crying, neither shall there be any more pain.' That is our comfort. In John 14:1-5, 'Let not your heart be troubled: ye believe in God, believe also in me. In my Father's house are many mansions: if it were not so, I would have told you. I go to prepare a place for you.'"

The preacher said, "Let us pray." He bowed his head and said, "Our Heavenly Father, help us know that no matter what, you love us. Help us all walk through this troublesome time in the valley of the shadow of death. Help us be aware of your presence. In the silence of this hour, speak to us of eternal things and the comfort of the Scriptures. We ask this all in the name of your son, Jesus. Amen."

The preacher continued and told the congregation that it had been good to sit with Wash's family to hear about his life. "They told me about how Wash loved his family and always looked out for them. He loved his mother and his grandfather. His dear mother told me he loved to go out picking blackberries in the summer and would beg her to make a blackberry cobbler. She said the blackberries stained his little fingers from picking the blackberries and stained his mouth from eating the cobbler. Oh, how he loved her cooking."

The preacher said it is never easy to lose a loved one. "So this afternoon, let us turn our hearts toward God, who is the giver of all comfort and the restorer of our souls. In hearing about Wash from several people who knew him, I know this was true with Wash. He embraced a relationship with Jesus Christ. Wash was a strong man, but Wash came to realize that he could never be strong enough on his own. Wash came to realize that there were things broken all around us. There is evil, pain, and suffering and there has to be an answer for that. He came to believe that the evil in this world was because of people turning away from God. Wash came to understand that Jesus came into the world to die on the cross for his sins. Jesus died in our place for all the wrong things we have ever done and will ever do."

The Bible says in Romans 6: 23, 'For the wages of sin is death; but the gift of God is eternal life through Jesus Christ our Lord. And friends, it is a gift that gives hope. We receive eternal life by putting our faith and trust in Jesus. Wash made Jesus the Lord of his life, and because of that, he could know now what David meant in Psalm 23, saying, 'He maketh me to lie down in green pastures: he leadth me beside the still waters. He restoreth my soul.' Wash knew that the Lord was the one who was going to sustain him."

"Life was hard for Wash. He struggled with pain and disappointment in his brief life on this earth. Sometimes things happened that he did not fully understand, but it encouraged him that one day all that was over and he could spend eternity in paradise."

"Friends, we must realize during this time of mourning there is good news! Through Jesus, death is not the end. We can know that we have eternal life with God. Heaven is an incredible place. No more death, no more goodbyes. Nor grief or any more sorrow. No more sin and no more pain. In Heaven, we will walk on streets of gold. There will be a family reunion, and God will reunite us with those who have gone on. In Heaven, we will experience a peace that is beyond comprehension. And we will be with Jesus. And we will finally see the great love of God in all of its glory."

The preacher told everybody to bow their heads as he closed. He prays, "Our Father, fulfill your promise that you will not leave your people comfortless, but will come to them. Reveal your love and grace to your grieving. Help them, O Lord, to turn to you in true faith, that, finding now the comfort of your presence. If anyone is in the room today who would like to place their faith and hope and trust in Jesus as their Lord and Savior, I ask that they would sincerely pray this prayer after me. Lord Jesus, I admit I am not perfect. I have made mistakes. But, I believe you died on the cross for my sins. Today, I ask your forgiveness as I commit my life to follow you as my Lord and Savior. Amen."

He gathered up his Bible and notes. He nodded for the pallbearers to stand and take the casket out of the church. The people at the church were so touched by the preacher's message to the family. Sounds of mothers moaning and the sounds of grief filled the church as tears streamed down the faces of many friends and family after the preacher spoke. Grief and sadness lingered heavily on the brows of those close to the family that had crowded the hot-humid church. Wash's mother had sat in the front row so she could hear every word the preacher said about her son. She twisted her handkerchief as tears flowed. She dreaded what was coming next. Pastor Murphy stood to lead the way out of the church, and a commotion and rumbling began throughout the church. An eerie feeling overtook everybody.

There were many people in the church. The building strained to hold all the mourners. Some people in the church started looking around, thinking they heard a faint rumbling. Dust seemed to fall from the rafters. The doors moved on their own, opening and closing slowly. The church started shaking and vibrating like the tail of a rattlesnake. Suddenly, a window slammed shut, shattering glass everywhere. The floor bellowed from the movement and the beams broke and fell off the corner, foundations slamming down like the force of a mighty oak tree crashing to the ground. The weight of the people crowding into the church made the structure give way to forces beyond anything one could imagine. It was as if it was a warning when the floor fell from the foundation a foot to the ground with a jolting force. It was an extremely frightening experience for everybody and it happened so quickly. People were clinging and gasping for each other for comfort as they fled the church. The terrified mourners were leaping out the shattered windows and cramming through the door, all trying to get out at once. Children were screaming for their mothers and clamping their arms around loved one's neck like a vise. Pandemonium had taken over, and it seemed like forever for things to settle down to return to the solemn task at hand.

Finally, they assembled back together around the opened grave for one last moment. The family and friends sang "Blessed Assurance" as the pallbearers held the ropes that slowly lowered the pine casket into the ground. He said, "Wash is with Jesus. We will be together again someday, and Jesus will take away all of our pain and suffering. Remember, in Revelation 21:4 that God shall wipe away all tears; and there will be no more death, sorrow, crying, or pain, and former things are passed away."

The preacher tried consoling the grieved and read from John 14, "Let not your heart be troubled: ye believe in God, believe also in me."

Reverend Murphy stood at the head of the casket and told everybody to bow their heads in prayer. He prayed, "O God, whose beloved Son took children into his arms and blessed them. Give us the grace to entrust Wash Smith to your never-failing care and love and bring us all to your heavenly kingdom; through Jesus Christ our Lord, who lives and reigns with you and the Holy Spirit, one God, now and forever. Amen."

He went around and shook hands with all the family around the grave before he left. Many people came up to Wash's mother to pay their respects to her, and either shook her hand or hugged her. She tried to smile but always thanked them for coming. As each person stopped and talked, many of the friends and relatives related stories about her son that spurred her memory and reminded her of things that happened during Wash's brief life. She heard from so many friends, and their stories broke her heart. She kept thinking if only she could go back to any of those times that were mentioned.

Death was for the elder, and the youth seemed to defy its clutches. From now on, she will have to rely on her memory for comfort. And the stories of her son filled her memory of him, his friends, and the area he lived.

CHAPTER 3:
THE SMITHS AND JUD WELLS

Beginning in 1892

In the Washington District of Banks County, Sue Ward and her grandparents lived. Sue lived a simple life, but one that was not without its tragedies. Her father died before she was born, and her mother died when she was six. She had to move in with her grandparents, and that by itself was a devastating change for a little six-year-old girl. Shortly afterward, her grandmother died when she was eight years old. That was many deaths in such a short time for a little girl. However, like everything else, she coped with the difficulties and lived her life the best she could.

As Sue matured, she grew into a petite, pretty young lady. One neighbor who lived down the narrow dirt road from them came to visit her grandfather and, over time, became fond of her. The man was about seventeen years older than Sue, and she was very naïve about situations of the sort. He came around to visit her often, and they had a child together in 1903 when she was still at home. The father took their baby boy home and raised him with his wife as their child. He had other children by women other than his wife that he took and raised. When he took Sue's son, she had no choice. From that point on, she made an oath to herself that her children would stay together no matter what.

Sue met Joseph Smith shortly after the child was born. Reverend Thomas T. Wells married them on May 20, 1905, in his home. They knew him at Leatherwood Baptist Church, where he was the preacher. The couple continued living in the Washington District and over the next few years, Sue and Joseph had several children. Ellen was the first to be born in 1906. The following year Horace was born and, over time, took on more and more of the family responsibility. Next came Curtis, Daisy, Flora, and Clifford.

Sometime around 1918, they moved to the Columbia District to farm and lived in one of the old houses on the Wells property. It was the old Wells home place and was about a quarter of a mile from where Jud Wells lived. The house was a single-story structure with a porch across the front, like many of the old houses in that area. It was unpainted, which gave the appearance of a cabin with weathered wood. They built the house using rocks for corner pillars and there were cracks in the floor large enough to see the chickens underneath.

The large kitchen was in the back of the house. There was a well that was covered with a shelter near the back door, where they would draw water for cooking and washing. Sue usually wore a long, simple dress that went down to her ankles. An apron always covered the skirt of the dress and tied it around her small waist. She would go out and lowered the bucket that was tied to a long rope into the well and wait for it to fill with water. She turned the handle at the end of the round piece of wood that had a rope attached. Most of the time, she had to use both hands to crank the handle in order to bring the filled water bucket to the top of the well. The bucket had to clear the opening into the well so the cover could slide over the hole and lower it to sit on the cover. You had to have another pail for the water to carry back to the kitchen. She would use the apron or the bottom of her dress as padding to her slender fingers when she lifted the heavy pail of water.

The Columbia District was a small farm community in the northeast corner of the county, just a short distance from the district where they use to live. Most of the people in the area lived and worked on farms as tenant farmers. Some neighbors owned their land in this district. Everybody in the community, one way or the other, lived on the land, worked for the Wells family, and traded at the Wells' store.

Jud Wells was the prominent landowner and business owner in this section of the county. His family owned hundreds of acres of land, several houses, a couple of distilleries, and the store there around that district. The people in Banks County valued the Wells family. There were preachers, merchants, politicians, teachers, and moonshiners in the family. Jud's father started the empire but died in the spring of 1922. He left everything to his family, and Jud and his sister were the only children left at home to oversee the operations. Jud did not marry, so taking over the management of the distilleries and farm seemed logical. Sometimes Jud ruled over the farmers with a stern hand and would be unsympathetic to their feelings. He had several brothers who could be just as ruthless toward him.

The farmers on the Wells' place lived there as tenant farmers. Tenant farmers worked on the land and had full control of the crops they grew and sold. They could use the money received from the sale of the crops for rent or merchandise in the store, or an arrangement could be a portion of the corn, cotton, and vegetables to be part of the rent.

Sharecroppers, unlike the tenant farmer, worked the land and planted crops the landowner wanted. They had no control over the crops planted or sold. The landowner shared a portion of their crop with the farmer. Since they grew the crops on the landlord's property, the owner took part of the crop in payment or money from its sale for the rent of the house. The debt had to be paid. Most families were simple folk who lived in a house on the land of a more prosperous neighbor. It was just a way of life and both profited.

After the Smith family moved, a daughter was born but died at age three in 1921 from chronic dysentery and colitis. The family buried her at Leatherwood Baptist Church next to loved ones. Four months later, another son was born.

Joseph started getting sick shortly before the youngest daughter was born in '24. The oldest daughter had helped with the chores in and around the house when she was home, but she married and moved somewhere in South Georgia around 1925. They packed up at two in the morning and left, telling nobody. They had one child, and Sue and Joseph deeply loved their only granddaughter. Nobody knew exactly where they were until several years later. Sue and Joseph were heartbroken. Joseph would never see his only grandchild again.

After twenty-one years of marriage, her faithful husband died September 6, 1926. It was seven in the morning when he passed from what the doctors said was acute carcinoma of the stomach. Following his death, Sue realized she was going to have another child.

Thoughts of her childhood were never far from her mind. Sue could not bear the thoughts of the same fate falling upon her children. Many days, her thoughts took her back to similar events in her own life as a child, but that was a long time ago and things are different now. She now had a family of her own. Horace vowed before his father died and to his mother that he would do everything in his power to keep the family together. He was the one Sue had to depend on now for help and support for the family. He pledged not to let them down.

The two oldest boys worked to help take care of the little ones and their mother by working on the property growing corn and making moonshine for Jud Wells., They were close to one of their friends age, Wash Smith, and they all worked together at the stills.

That made eight children and one on the way. All her children were dear to her, and they did their best to help make her life easier by working on the farm and doing whatever was necessary after their father died. She instilled in their minds the importance of taking care of the family and protecting them from influences that tore them apart. Her family must survive.

Sue had to fend for herself and her children. Jud and Sue were close to the same age and, over time, were very fond of each other. He made sure she had a place to live and food to eat, especially since her husband had died. The family had lived for several years on the farm. Jud visited often to make sure her family was well.

He came in to visit and would ask, "Do you need anything? Have you got enough food?"

Sue always said, "Yes, we have enough." She would thank him for coming by and checking.

Jud would ask Sue about the kids and let her know if they did anything around the farm that might make her worry about one of them getting hurt or into something they should not be getting into. One day, he came in and told Sue that Daisy and Wash were seeing each other. Sue did not know that her daughter was seeing Wash, but Daisy had been seeing him for several months. Jud told her that Wash was not a favorable influence on her and should discourage the two from seeing each other. Sue asked Daisy about what Jud had told her, and Daisy said they were just friends.

Jud was a very stern and often indifferent man to those who worked for him, but Sue and her children saw his compassionate side. Sue was an excellent cook, and Jud would come by for a bite to eat and would occasionally stay for dinner. Sometimes she fried fatback and used the grease to cook dried green beans, called leather britches. The family picked green beans and strung the beans on twine, nailed behind the wood cook stove to dry. When you wanted to cook some, you had to soak them overnight in water to soften them up. The next morning she poured the water off and cooked in fatback grease and water for a couple of hours on low heat. The farmers dried other various types of beans, like black-eyed peas, and they dried apples from the trees around the property. They dried the food to use later. Her meals might be simple, but nobody complained about how tasty they were. She never turned a visitor away who came around eating time and no one refused her cooking.

CHAPTER 4:
WASH AND DAISY

Daisy lived on the farm with her mother, brothers, and sisters and enjoyed living there because others her age lived close by. She had grown up with all the area children since they all went to the same school or church. Work was hard for everyone, and they enjoyed time together whenever they could. Going to the same church made it easy to catch up on all the news around the Columbia District, and an occasional meeting at Jud's store where they shared candy or bubble gum with others. Daisy was getting interested in some of the local boys and often met up with Wash, who was a few years older.

Wash was an eighteen years old, good-looking country boy with brown hair, blue eyes, and about five and a half feet tall. He was a meek and humble boy when he was around family. He loved and cared for them deeply, but he could be short-tempered if anybody did him or his family and friends wrong. For the last several months, he had been living with Delmar Chitwood, who hired Wash to work and grow a crop on his farm. The two of them made that arrangement around Christmas of '27.

Being outdoors was one of Wash's most desired things to do. He hunted with the Chitwood boy's double-barrel shotgun, which was the same gun he used to guard the moonshine stills. Wash was young and some might say he could be a little overconfident and short-tempered, and sometimes he swaggered around like a young bantam rooster. He was arrogant and independent, but his family was important to him, which was true for all the families in the community. Wash worked hard at everything he did for his family.

Like all young boys his age in the area, his thoughts went to the usual feelings of a growing teenager. Working, hunting, and dating occupied much of his time. He was quite fond of the girls around the community, but he favored Daisy. She was sixteen, and they enjoyed each other's company. She was as pretty as he was handsome. Daisy was petite, like her mother. She was small but worked hard around the farm.

Some people may have disapproved of Wash and Daisy dating, but Jud was the only one anybody knew for sure. Daisy had not told Wash what Jud told her mom and thought it best to not bother him with those details now. She knew they worked together and best not to cause any trouble when it was unnecessary.

Wash and Daisy were in love and had been dating for about a year. They were planning on getting married. Most of their friends knew the two were in love and only a matter of time before they expected to wed. Just before Christmas, Daisy told their plans to Billie Joe Brown at Leatherwood Baptist Church. Daisy told her she did not think they could afford a church wedding so they could either get the preacher at Leatherwood Baptist or go to a Justice of the Peace. Daisy told Billie Joe that Jud Wells' father, who was the preacher at Leatherwood for many years, had married her mother and father back in 1905 and her sister in 1921. If they got married at the church, the pastor there now could do the ceremony. Daisy kept thinking about her conversation with Billie Joe concerning these wedding plans for the next several weeks.

After a while, Daisy finally told Wash what Jud said to her mother about them seeing each other. Jud told her mother that Wash was not a proper influence for her. Some people knew Jud had told people Wash had better stop seeing Daisy, or else. Wash took that as a deadly threat, and the relationship between Wash and Jud suffered. Afterward, he always felt uneasy around Jud and thought he had to step easy when around him. Wash and Daisy did not hide their love for one another. Like most teenagers their age, they continued seeing each other.

What was Jud's reason for making such a statement about Wash? As far as Wash knew, he and Jud were good friends and could not see in his mind why Jud did not want them to be happy. Jud was old enough to be her father and the possibility of him being fond of Daisy was not conceivable to Wash. He did not let that thought tangle in his mind until Daisy told him Jud had made an improper advancement toward her.

She did not go into any details about the advancement, but why she did not tell him confused Wash. From that point, Wash was very suspicious of Jud, very protective of his relationship with Daisy, and always watchful to protect his life. The thoughts twisted his mind on what to do. Why did his friend make such a vicious statement to his girlfriend's mother?

CHAPTER 5:
LIFE IN THECOMMUNITY
AND MOONSHINE

Wash was ready to earn his way in the world. He worked hard on the farm, growing crops for the landowner or guarding moonshine stills for the Wells family. The dangers of working the stills always concerned his mother. She was not one to be overbearing and demanding, nor dominating and controlling. A day did not go by that she did not worry about what he was doing. He tried to console her, but he did not want her to fret over him or make a fuss about him working. He was in a hurry to grow up and be on his own. Having money in his pocket to get a few of the things he wanted or his mother needed was a feeling that made him feel good about himself.

Wash and several of his friends worked the stills that Jud Wells owned. When Wash worked the stills, he always had a shotgun and carried it just about everywhere he went. It may have been more out of habit to have it than a need. He needed to protect the still and needed to hunt for food. He was ready for just about anything that came around. At the still, there would always be an escape route, and getting caught meant no work. He was young and fast, so escaping the clutches of the revenuer was something Wash did not let bog his mind.

Life during the 1920s was difficult for most people in the mountains. Everybody had to grow their food and would barter their milk, butter, buttermilk, eggs, or chickens for harder to get items like salt, sugar, or flour. They grew corn as food for the family, the livestock, and the moonshine. The South had its hardships for more than a decade. It was no fault of any one person.

One cannot control the weather and a severe drought in the area made it hard to raise crops in abundance. Cotton was no exception. With the prices of cotton per bale falling, it took more and more cotton each year to make ends meet. So the drought produced less cotton and the demand for it was less. The increased use of synthetic fiber forced families to look for other ways to make sure the family had the essentials just to live. Corn grew easier and had various uses than other crops. The entire plant served its purpose to help feed everyone involved, whether man or beast.

Other crops fell into the same situation as cotton. Less rain produced fewer crops. Many of the larger landowners supplemented their income by producing something hard to get and risky to make. They did not want to be the one at risk, so tenants on their land took the risk and everybody profited. Making moonshine was common knowledge in the county. That was just a way of life in the area. Calling it a distillery may have been how it eased the minds of those working one but did not change the fact that getting caught meant dire consequences. Many tenants took that chance since making moonshine made up the difference in what growing crops had failed to produce.

Their ancestors brought moonshine to the Appalachian Mountains of North Georgia. Increased production of alcoholic beverages directly resulted from the prohibition of bootleg liquor. A federal law made it illegal to manufacture, sell, transport, and buy any form of alcohol. Because moonshine was a much-desired commodity, the production of the substance was worth the risk. It made a quick twelve dollars a gallon for the bootlegger, and one run could make about twenty-gallon. That was a lot of money for those who were struggling to stay alive, anyway. The enormous profits lured the distiller to take the risk associated with making moonshine. Getting caught could cause a $5000.00 fine or a maximum of one year in prison, or both. In 1929, the risk increased to $10,000 in fines and a prison sentence of up to five years. It did not deter those around the area from stopping production.

Moonshiners set up the stills around the hills near a water source and off the beaten path so it was hard for the revenuer to locate. They operated the stills in the moonlight so it would be hard to see the smoke coming from the still when they used wood. Smoke from a still gave away its location if the revenuer could see smoke rising where there was not a house. Most of the time, the moonshiner worked the stills at night so the revenuer could not see the smoke. Working during the daytime was riskier, and it was safer to use coke because it did not smoke.

Moonshine brought in more money, and the tenant farmers and top officials in the government enjoyed drinking the illegal substance. The prohibition era ran as long as the drought. They did not frown on brewing it for medical use. Most houses had some in a Mason jar for a cold or a cough, and the law said nothing about having medicine at home to cure the family. Revenuer did not even think that much mattered and turned their legal eyes away from the moonshine. It is when they jarred forty quarts or more when the revenuer tried to locate the still and close the operation. The Wells family had several distilleries around the area and employed twelve or thirteen workers.

Moonshiners never put more than one still at a location. If those pesky revenuers found one and destroyed it, making it impossible to use, it would not stop production completely. Production may have slowed down the supply for a while. The moonshiner worked at another still until they could repair it and moved to a better, more hidden location. Most of the time the revenuer sat and watched, especially if the evidence around a still looked as though someone had been working one. The apprehension of a moonshiner was more important than destroying one. Moonshiners were smart for keeping an eye out for a revenuer. When they returned to work a still, they scanned the area for any evidence of a visitor. Usually, one worker stood watch with a shotgun in case the wrong person came around prying.

Everybody knew who the revenuers were and even the children kept the secret of what goes on in those out-of-the-way spots around their home. Keeping silent was important. One did not go around telling what went on in the family. Everybody in the family did what was necessary to make sure the family had what they needed to live. Jud left the risk-taking to the tenant farmers to run the stills and deliver the goods. He did not want to risk being arrested for making moonshine. Jud passed that honor to some other worker on the farm. He felt they could not replace him.

Jud used the youth in the area to run the stills and distribute the prohibited product. Wash, Oliver Brock, and a man named Dudley Ayers operated one still. Nobody knew too much about Mr. Ayers, only that he helped at the still. Jud hired him to work. Oliver was a friend of Jud's. He lived upon Currahee Mountain not far above Jud, on the line of Banks and Stephens Counties. Sue's oldest sons Horace and Curtis Smith and Will Freeman's son Calloway ran the other still. Will Freeman was a tenant neighbor that lived down an old dirt road about three hundred yards from the Wells store. All the workers lived close together and made it easy to get to the hiding spots and work at the stills. Wash guarded both stills and some of the other boys transported the quarts of liquor to buyers and speakeasies in the cities.

Transporting moonshine had its difficulties. Horace and Curtis had a car they used to haul moonshine to anyone who purchased the elixir. Curtis was a first-rate mechanic and kept the engines in top running order. He had learned to tinker on the old cars once he was old enough to drive. Horace would drive and was careful not to get into a situation if it meant trouble. The car had curtains hanging in the back windows, and they put additional leaf springs under to raise the car higher. The extra weight of the quart jars of moonshine weighed the car down, and the extra springs kept the car from sinking too low to the ground once they loaded the cargo.

Everybody was so used to seeing that car around town nobody questioned its use. It was just the Smith boy's old car. Both were very careful any time they went out in the car. They fixed the car so that if they put a load of moonshine in the car's trunk. It looked like they had not loaded down the car with anything. The two of them had to be careful. Who would help their mother with her responsibilities if they were caught?

CHAPTER 6:
THE BEGINNING OF THE END

Tuesday, January 3, 1928

The New Year started like any day in the community, with not much going on that was any different from any other day in the lives of those that lived in the area. Today turned out to be a little different in more ways than usual. It was twenty-one degrees and a cold windy day in the mountains with a light covering of snow. Sue said it was hog-killing weather and everybody was up getting that task underway. The weather had to be cold for killing a hog, so the temperature had to be below 40 degrees. The lack of electricity and a way to keep the meat from spoiling meant it had to be done when the weather was right. They cured hog meat by preserving it by salting the meat down, and farms had a smokehouse to hold the meat. They rarely used larger animals like a steer or a cow as a food source because it was harder to preserve than a hog. A cow provided milk and butter for the family and would be too valuable as a commodity to use as a food source. They cooked small animals like squirrels, rabbits, possum, or chickens since they could consume them in one meal.

When killing a hog, building an outside fire to heat water in a cast iron wash tub started the process. Getting the pulley hung in the tree to get the hog up so the blood could drain came next. Placing a well-aimed shot to the head began the chore, and at that point, there was no turning back. Killing a hog was a chore that happened only when the weather was cold enough and was not one the farmers did often, but the everyday chores still had to be done.

Each day began like all cold wintry days in the mountains of north Georgia. Morning chores were getting done and gathering wood for the stove was an everyday task. They built most houses with no way to keep out the cold. It was not uncommon to see the chickens through the cracks in the floor under the house. At night, the fire went down and the rooms got cold. Piles of homemade quilts made from the clothes children had outgrown were on the beds to keep out the freezing cold.

The first chore of the day would be to get a fire in the wood cook stove to warm the house and start breakfast. Sue made biscuits with hog lard, flour, and buttermilk, and cooked in the oven. She cooked bacon and eggs and used the grease from the bacon with flour and milk made gravy. Hearty breakfasts were common on the farms since work was hard. It was not uncommon to start before daybreak, milking the cow and collecting eggs for the day. One boy milked the cow while his sister gathered eggs and collected them in the apron they wore to protect one of the few dresses she had. As one walked out to the barn, it was easy to see the wispy clouds of breath float upward.

Work continued throughout the day, leaving little time to relax. Water had to be brought in from the well to cook with, drink, wash dishes, bathe and wash clothes. Keeping water on the stove to heat when needed was simply a chore to be done. Just for the sake of making life a little easier ended up being somebody's chore for the day. Once the start of the day began, it was work till bedtime. Just because it was cold outside, it was not enough to stop getting what needed to be done to take care of one's family.

Many times, someone would get up early and go hunting to get a rabbit or squirrel for breakfast. Wash was out hunting early this morning with Clarence Simpson, one of his best friends. The two of them walked the country roads in the area and would talk about events in the community. Clarence already knew what Jud had said to Daisy's mother for Wash to stay away. Clarence tried to stay away from that topic. Wash could not help but worry. Wash wanted to go by Jud's house to ask him about what he had told Sue. Jud's Sister Minnie was the only one there and told Wash he was not home and did not know where he was. Minnie could tell Wash was upset and told him to leave Jud alone and not hurt him. Clarence left after that and went home, and Wash continued to hunt with his dog.

Jud and Will had met down at Sue's house around sunrise to help her butcher a hog, and Will killed it. They knew she had been sick, and they helped. It was between one and one thirty when Will left for home, and he was not sure when Jud left. He passed Wash about a hundred and fifty yards from Jud's house, where he was on top of a brush pile trying to scare out a rabbit. He carried his hunting gun and his dog followed him. From this time on and for the next several hours, lives were going to be changed in a way no one could realize until much later.

After passing Wash, Will walked slowly down the old dirt road and stopped at his house. He got a bite to eat before he went out again to check on the still. Will had seen Wash earlier on his way to Sue's but ran into him again, with Oliver at one of the stills. Everybody got to drinking the brew and may have had a little too much of the manufactured substance. Once one started drinking the beverage, stopping was hard. Oliver left the still first but left Wash and Will there. Wash had little to eat all day and was getting hungry. He asked Will several times to go with him to the Wells' store to get something to eat. Will finally decided that he wanted some smoking tobacco, so the two of them left for the store. They stopped by Will's house and Miss Minnie Wells stopped there to visit with his wife. The two of them stayed for about half an hour before walking to the store. It was about three hundred yards from Will's house to the store. Wash called out for Jud, and he was at his house which was about twelve or thirteen yards away. Will and Wash did not go up to the house but stayed outside near the store.

Jud asked, "What would you have?"

Wash said, "I'm hungry. Can you bring a bowl and two spoons to the store?"

Jud said, "Let me get my hat, and I'll be right out." He went back into the house and came out with the bowl and spoons, and Oliver followed. He had gone to Jud after he left the still and had been there for about an hour. It was a cold day, and they were in the house by the hearth warming. Oliver told Jud he had killed a hog the day before, and Jud wanted to negotiate a price for a hog for himself. The two of them left for the country store without settling on a price.

CHAPTER 7:
THE STORE

The Wells had a store that was about twenty-five or thirty feet from the two-story house that Jud and Minnie lived in. If anyone came up to the store, it did not take Jud long to get over there to help. The store was a small wood-framed building about twelve or thirteen feet long and about ten feet wide. They painted it white with a front porch that was close to the ground. A single board about six inches wide covered the opening between the floor and the ground. Well-worn boards covered the porch and, like all wooden floors, made a sound when walking across. Summers could be hot in the south, and the covered porch served as a gathering place for men to talk. A bench, chair, or the side of the porch provided a place to sit and talk about the weather, prices of crops, politics, revenuers, and news about events in and around the store.

Inside, the store was like any other old country store in the area with counters and shelves inside. The counter started a few feet from the door and ran down the left side across the back and just enough room for you to walk behind. The counter was about six feet long and waist high. A cold potbelly stove stood off to the right side of the counter and a square wooden table with chairs was in the middle of the floor. People could sit and talk or eat crackers and cheese or play a friendly game of checkers. Behind the counter were shelves that went almost to the ceiling with canned goods of just about anything you would want. There was coffee, sugar, salt and pepper, flour, hard candy, and bubble gum. There were canned oysters, canned tomatoes, and peaches. He had honey and molasses, crackers, cheese, and tobacco. There were plows and metal goods like nails, along with clothing, playing cards, guns, and ammunition. Tenant farmers brought in extra meat, vegetables, eggs, butter, and milk to sell or trade, but most people had those anyway at home and used to barter with neighbors who needed what they had.

Will and Wash got to the store about four to four thirty in the evening, and they found the front door locked. Oliver and Jud came from the house with the key to unlock the door, and everyone walked in about the same time. As always, Wash was carrying the same old double-barreled shotgun that he had earlier in the day. He had been hunting and was on his way back from the woods to get some more shells for his gun. As he entered the store, he propped the gun up against the counter next to the door. Will told him he needed to lay the gun down. If that thing fell over, it could shoot someone. Wash picked it up and laid the weapon down on the counter.

The conversation around the old table between the men was just about what one expected when they got together. They discussed the events of that cold-wintry day. Jud and Will had been talking about killing the hog.

Will looked at Jud, "Did you salt the old lady's hog down?"

Jud said nothing. He just continued with his work. Oliver sat on a bag of meal or bran and argued with Will about who stole a gallon of moonshine from the still. Wash was not offering a lot to the conversation. He was still uneasy about the statement Jud had made to Sue. Jud went behind the counter and got some canned tomatoes off the shelf. Wash bought some shells with a five-dollar bill. Jud gave him change back, and he opened the tomatoes with his pocketknife and poured them into the bowl. He cut them up with that same old knife.

Wash threw the spoon down after tasting the tomatoes, "These things have got ice in 'em!"

Jud offered to take the tomatoes to the house and warm them since the potbelly stove stood unused that day, but Wash said he would rather have canned oysters instead. Jud reached around and got a can and cut it open. He set the oysters down by the bowl.

While at the store, none of the men had any more moonshine to drink. Will and Oliver were in a heavy discussion about a missing gallon of moonshine and were not paying any attention to what Wash and Jud were saying. The conversation between Wash and Jud had been at a strain for the last couple of months. Wash knew Jud had plenty of money and feared he would have him arrested and sent to prison, so he kept quiet about his fears. The two of them said very little to each other when they worked together. Wash felt Jud was always mad at something he had done, and Jud would cuss him for anything Wash did.

There had been little talk between Wash and Jud when they got into the store. Jud finally told Wash he needed to stay away from Daisy. This opened up a chance for Wash to confront Jud about his comment to see if he meant what he said.

Wash nervously said, "Did you mean what you said when you said I had to stay away from Daisy." His voice got louder and louder as he continued in a rage yelling at Jud, and said, "Daisy was going to be your woman and if she wasn't, you would kill me."

Jud yelled at the top of his voice, only two words. "Hell yes!"

Wash angrily started toward the door to leave the store after that remark and got his gun to leave.

Jud bellowed out in a heated fit of anger, "Yes, hell! I meant it. I'll do it right now!"

As Jud made this comment, he was reaching under the counter. That action convinced Wash that Jud was grabbing for his gun. He thought Jud was going to carry out his threat, and Wash could not let that happen. He had to protect himself.

Suddenly, there was a loud explosion from a gun, and everybody drew their attention to the actions. They turned around to see what had happened. Wash fired the gun, hitting Jud in the neck. Jud grabbed his neck. Wash was about eight feet away when he fired the fatal shot. Jud fell back against a box behind the counter. Will ran out the door and Wash went behind the counter and throwed the gun down on him, thinking he was still reaching for his gun, and fired again, hitting Jud in the back of the head. During this time in the 1920s, it was common for hunters to say to throw a gun at something meant that he was aiming.

Oliver was still sitting near the counter when the commotion started. He followed Will out the door as soon as he could and was about fifty yards down the road when he heard the second shot. That second shot hit Jud in the head. There was no way for anyone to survive such a wound. The two of them heard nothing being said to have led to the deadly incident. Jud reached under the counter and Wash took the action as being a threat. The split second Wash fired the deadly shot changed his brief life forever. One could not bring back the fatal shell that ended Jud's life. That sight etched in Wash's mind caused him to panic.

Wells Store Columbia District Banks County

CHAPTER 8:
THE HUNT

Wash fled the scene like a hunted rabbit. The closest house that offered him refuge would be that of Sue Smith. With all the excitement that he had been through, he entered so quickly that he accidentally fired a shot that went through the ceiling of the house. The sudden explosion from the gun unnerved those in the house, and Sue fainted, needing help to get up. Horace and Calloway Freeman, a friend, had gotten home about four or five from Baldwin. They left about eight or nine o'clock in the morning on their way to pick up sugar, quart jars, and medicine for Horace's mother. With Sue being sick and fainted from all the excitement, she asked Calloway to get Wash out of the house and go with him to get some medicine for her. Wash had already told what had happened earlier and decided it best to seek cover somewhere less obvious and left with Calloway.

As he passed the store, several people had gathered around the front of the crime scene, trying to piece together the mayhem. One look at Wash sent those congregating outside scattering, thinking one of them may be his next victim.

Wash was panicking about where to go and what to do. He went home to Delmar Chitwood's house and listened to the gramophone for about an hour, trying to relax but was restless the entire time. Wide awake for fear of falling asleep, he paced the floor tirelessly. Believing it a dead giveaway to anybody looking for him, he hurriedly charges out, trying to find a place of safety. Wash came around the curve in the road and unexpectedly came upon the posse looking for him. It had been six or seven hours since the shooting, and the hunt for him was getting intense.

S. J. Whelchel, sheriff of Banks County, formed a posse with P. C. Wilbanks from Habersham County. There were several deputies out on that cold winter night. As they cut around a hill, the posse could hear something coming out of the dark surroundings. The posse could not be exactly sure who might come toward the front of them, so they had to be vigilant in what they did. The posse and Wash could hear the rustling of brush. Wash had a hard time seeing the posse huddled against the bank in the gully next to the road even though the moon was almost full. The posse heard both barrels being cocked.

Wash yelled out into the dark, "Boys, I ain't got a damn word to say. If you got anything to say, say it now!"

The sheriff tried to keep his eyes on Wash and distract him, to jump and capture him. Wash was told to drop the gun. He whirled around and fired both barrels, one, then the other. The sheriff fired a shot and ran to capture Wash. The posse followed with shots toward him. Wash was too quick and escaped into the night, dropping his gun in the cold moonlight. His escape was not without its dangers.

When Wash met up with the posse, they wounded him. He got shot in one arm and broke both bones in the other arm. Wash went to Wiley Brown's house between ten and midnight and woke him from sleep. Wiley went after Dr. Holly to come and mend Wash's wounds. Exhausted and finally able to rest, Wash fell asleep only for a short time. About two in the morning, the posse came to Mr. Brown's house checking for Wash. He led the sheriff to where Wash slept. The sheriff pulled the covers back. Wash, worn out from the chaos of the day, did not resist. The sheriff ordered Wash to get up, and he told the sheriff he could not because they had shot him. Wash pleaded for them not to be so rough.

The sheriff arrested Wash immediately. His flight ended, and thoughts of the day raced through his mind. The county jail held Wash until the courts completed the paperwork for the arraignment of a trial. He had plenty of time to think back over the past several hours and days. Wash kept thinking that the shooting had to be in self-defense otherwise; he ended his future.

News reports of the incident had already hit the papers. An Atlanta paper had an article about a posse seeking a farmer's slayer. The clipping states that a well-known farmer of the county died from a gunshot wound and had not received details of the killing. Few families in the area got The Atlanta Constitution, so news from the paper went unnoticed. The local paper had articles about the murder and case, but it did not report as much of the news that the larger newspaper did. Wash's family held on to every article they could get and carefully clipped it from the newspaper and saved it to read later. The family collected the articles and put them away in old Bibles pressed between the pages or put aside deep in a camelback chest in an envelope to collect any more that may arrive.

CHAPTER 9:
JAIL

The sheriff held Wash in the jail in Homer, Georgia, across the road from the courthouse. The jail was a two-story structure built in 1906. Four cells were upstairs and two holding cells. A trapdoor gallow was upstairs they used for hangings. The jailer's office and quarters were downstairs.

Wash, convinced that he fired those two shots in self-defense, truly felt Jud would take his life from him if he had not protected himself. He had pondered what Jud had said many times that he should not see Daisy anymore. The more he thought about it, the more it convinced him he was right. He now had plenty of time to think about his family, his girlfriend, and his actions. Nothing at the moment changed where he sat. He had to prove that the events happening terrified him for his life and that he had to protect himself.

Jud uttered those fateful words, "Or else!"

Those two words kept coming to his mind repeatedly. He could not get the words to go away. A haunting feeling cloaked him. Time passed slowly for Wash, sitting in the jail. He had plenty of time to think about the past and plan for the future. His family was searching for a lawyer to represent him in court, and he waited patiently for the news about when the trial would begin. Wash spent hour after hour locked up in the old jail. He tried not to think about how hopeless things were and knew that his only chance would be to prove self-defense. Wash was used to freedom and to come and go as he wanted. Being in a small cell by himself wore immensely on his mind and body.

Wash thought back about growing up and when times were simple. He remembered that school was not the easiest for him and would get distracted thinking about hunting, fishing, or just being outside. School lessons did not always seem important but got the basic elements of education. Broad River School was the closest place for the children to get an education. Wash had to walk to school like all the other children in the area. Those in the Columbia District went to the same school down on Broad River. It was easier for them to cut through the woods and follow the river to the school. The children had to cross the river once they were close enough to get to the school, which sat on a hill just above the river. It was a one-room schoolhouse that housed grades one to seven. The teacher's desk was up front, with an individual desk for each student.

The school was like all other one-room schoolhouses. One big room with all grades together. It looked more like a church than a school, but it served the purpose. The bell was in a steeple with a long rope hanging down for the teacher to pull, to let the students know when to come in for the beginning of school or recess. Wash always said that one of the Smith boys climbed up to the bell and tied the rope to a nail so the teacher could not ring the bell to end recess. Nobody ever snitched on them, and it happened more times than the teacher thought was funny. Most of the kids took school seriously, but a lot of the boys would stay out and go hunting for the day. It was rare that they stayed home or went hunting, but some stayed out more than others did. Wash was mischievous. But mostly, he was not a problem in school. Sometimes, on his way back home from school, he would stop and fish in the river below the school before he went home. Wash helped clean the fish he caught and watched them being cooked in an old black cast-iron skillet. Even though he was young, he was taking care of his family.

The county set the trial of The State VS Wash Smith for the March term in Banks County. The county scheduled the trial for March 19, 1928, before the Honorable W.W. Stark, Superior Court Judge of Banks County. Hopefully, he could get an honest lawyer who would prove his innocence. Surely, someone could find one. Caleb Smith, Wash's grandfather, hired Finnley Barrett and Early C. Stark as his counsel for the trial and built a case for self-defense. The lawyer and defendant spent many hours interviewing Wash for the case.

Occasionally, he got a visit from his lawyer, but it was those visits from his family that gave him the most hope and pleasure. He savored every second they were there. He always asked about how his mother was doing. The situation he was in made his heart heavy whenever he thought about her. His greatest desire would be to hug her and tell her just how much he loved her. Doing that through these bars that held him would not ease the hurt he had in his heart. It was important to him to know that all his family was well.

Of course, he always wanted to find out about Daisy. As time went on, stories about Daisy became fewer and fewer. It was as if she had moved on with her life without him, and Wash could not understand why. It might have been that Wash did not want to understand, but deep down he knew that their life together would never happen. He grieved over losing her, but he was not in a situation to change that fact. Wash spent many hours reliving his times with her and dreamed of the time they were together and the good times they had in planning the day they would marry. He woke up in a sweat only to realize where he was sleeping. Wash had a more despairing situation to deal with at the moment. He forced himself to not dwell on his losses and focus on his present situation.

The Jail Homer, Georgia

CHAPTER 10:
HORACE AND CURTIS'
BUSINESS

Horace wanted to check on Wash when he went into Homer to get sugar and other supplies and to run a few errands for his mom. He got there about the middle of the morning. After finishing the chores that brought him to town, Horace wanted to have a brief visit with Wash to let him know about home. Wash was glad to hear about the family, but he had very little to say to him.

Horace went downstairs and got to talking to Sheriff Whelchel on the first floor after his visit. With the usual greetings and conversation one would have with the sheriff, he told Horace about some activities around the county that involved the law. He told about one of the neighbor's cows getting out and getting caught in a fence at a farm in the Hollingsworth area of the county. He said he had confiscated a still from a bootlegger the sheriff had been trying to catch for some time. The sheriff put the still in an old storage building behind his house. He told Horace he was going to be out of town for the next few days and told him not to bother the still.

Horace and Curtis made plans on starting up a still of their own, and they wanted to operate it with nobody helping. The two of them would not have to share any of the profits with anybody. Since the incident between Wash and Jud, things around the farm had drastically changed. Making moonshine required a different approach since Jud died. The extra money from the new still helped with expenses at home.

Horace and Curtis went back into town late that evening after the sheriff left on his trip to retrieve the still he had mentioned. They found the outbuilding where the sheriff told them it would be and took it out piece by piece to stash it in the old car they had fixed up. The curtains in the back window hid most of the still, but the size of it was not what they had expected. They first thought it was a 20 gallon still, but it turned out to be a 50-gallon one instead. They had trouble getting it all to fit into their car. Rearranging the parts to fit better, many of the copper coils were sticking out around the car through the curtains and windows. Satisfied that it made the trip to a new hiding place, they started down through the middle of the town. The curtains were flapping in the wind, and the tubing cut the wind from the car, making a strange sound going down the road. Nobody paid much attention to them and just thought it was something for the farm or parts for an old car that Curtis always seemed to work on.

They set the still up on Broad River in what they called Brown's Bottoms in a shallow cave. Horace and Curtis had learned how to make moonshine while working at the stills for Jud. He had taught them how to make some of the best liquor of anybody in the county, and it was easy to dispose of the jars of moonshine. A lot of buyers from as far away as Atlanta had heard of the brew they made and requested their batch over others. They needed quart Mason jars for their moonshine, and finding jars for home canning was hard and forced families to dry the food rather than can it. Not a word was ever said to Horace or Curtis about the missing still. The sheriff later told them he did not know who took it. They would leave a quart of moonshine around the courthouse every once in a while as payment for the still. Horace and Curtis always suspected he knew they took it, but he never said a word. The sheriff knew they had a lot of responsibility for helping their mother take care of the other children.

CHAPTER 11:
THE TRIAL(PART 2)

March 1928

The county held the trial during the March term of the Superior Court on March 19, 1928. Wash expected it to take several days to present all the facts and listen to all the testimony of the witnesses. He was confident that his lawyer would prove a not guilty verdict to murder, and voluntary manslaughter would be obvious. The state was pushing for a murder conviction and was going to recommend the penalty to the maximum of the law. How could self-defense end him up with a death penalty charge? He had to depend on his lawyers to set the facts straight in the trial. It was up to them to plead to the jurors for them to recommend a lesser sentence after the lawyers presented the facts laid out before the jury. He hoped that the trial went smoothly and without a hitch.

Wash got up early the morning of the trial to a chilly morning of about thirty-seven degrees. He dressed warmly in a suit and tie. Wash had trouble getting the tie to look and hang the way it should, and the sheriff helped him fix it. Wash thought he had a lot more experience tying them, having to wear one to work every day with his uniform. He was glad to have the help, as nervous as he was. It was important to present him as a clean-cut, respectable citizen. He sauntered to his awaiting trial, and his nervousness showed on his face and mannerisms. The courthouse was just across the road from the jail. Gathered outside the building were hundreds of on-lookers. Curious people wanted to know what was going to happen. Their curiosity was enough for them to stop their usual routine for the day to attend the trial.

Banks County courthouse was a grand-looking building built in 1860 out of bricks made on-site from the red clay around the area. The two-story building had offices on the lower floor, and the courtroom and the judge's chamber were on the second floor, accessible only by a double staircase outside the building. The front of the building had four columns to support a covered roof that sheltered the stairs.

Upstairs, the courtroom took up more than half of the floor and had a drab look to it. At the very back of the courtroom, there were two doors on each side of the judge's desk. The judge's chamber was through the door to the left of the judge containing law books as references and the jury room to the right. A toilet was available in the rooms for the judge and jury.

In the main room, the judge's bench was a raised platform above the general court that appeared to be built into the wall. The witness stand was just to the right. The jury box was located to the right of the judge's bench, separated by a banister about waist high. It had an unobstructed view of all the proceedings. In front of the judge's bench, there were two tables with wooden chairs, one for the State and the other for Wash and his attorneys. Wash was to the right of the judge and the State at the other table. It looked like any other trial that had ever taken place in the old courthouse. This time Wash Smith was being tried.

Wash's mother and grandfather came to the trial. The courtroom was already getting crowded, and they were glad they got there early so they could get seats close to him. The sheriff escorted Wash into the room to his chair. When he turned into the aisle, he could see them together. His mother, wearing a simple dress that went to the floor and a simple hat, reached out her hand toward her son to touch him one more time, but the sheriff pulled him back and would not let him get close to her. He could tell by the look on his mother's face that she had been crying. He wanted so desperately to comfort her. Her father put his arm around her to hold her up, and she buried her face in his arm. It hurt him to see her worry. He tried to let her know things will be better later and for her not to worry. That was not in her nature not to be concerned about her children.

The court proceedings began like any other case in the courthouse. The bailiff instructed the court by saying, "Please rise. This court of the Superior Court of Banks County is now in session."

Court opened with the lawyers for both sides standing and telling the judge that he was ready, and they addressed the judge with "Your Honor." The jury selection for the case began and Wash thought this would take a long time and waited in his chair for the process to be completed. More than likely, every person on the panel knew one or both of the men involved in the case. It seemed to be a long-drawn-out process for Wash, but both lawyers wanted to make sure they selected the right person for a juror. A jury selected that could be unbiased in deciding of such great importance. Especially since the two sides wanted such drastic differences in the trial's outcome. The state wanted the maximum sentence and nothing less. Wash wanted voluntary manslaughter and nothing more. He had not denied that what he did was wrong. A person does not simply kill another human being for no reason. Wash thought that self-defense could never result in a harsh penalty and that would protect a person from such a punishment. Wash patiently waited for the selection of the jury to be made and his lawyer assured him that finding the right person was a necessary step in his case to get the results they hoped to receive.

With this Wash's heart pounded so hard, he was sure everybody could hear it, and the proceedings began. He struggled to swallow and fought back his emotions because his mother was there. Don't worry, he thought. It will be fine. He wanted to turn and look at her but decided that would be too much for both.

The lawyers for the State and the defense needed time to make sure the witnesses were ready and prepared to be questioned by both sides for the court to continue and for all those not chosen to be on the jury a chance to leave. Few of those not chosen left the building. They were just as curious as many of the others that came just to watch.

The county planned for the jury to eat at the boarding house of Mrs. Linda Shubert for dinner at noon. As the twelve jurors were preparing to leave, the judge instructed them to stay together as a group. With so many people in attendance at the trial and hundreds of people milling around outside discussing the facts in the case, the jurors needed to stay together. The plaintiff grouped the jurors to leave because it is customary that a juror has no contact with outside influences. Both parties wanted a fair trial and outside ideas might sway a panel member. The judge interrupted the schedule for the court and announced the noon recess. This break gave the jurors a chance to get something to eat while the lawyer prepared the next part of the trial.

Before the jurors left for the noon recess, the bailiff took them into the two rooms behind the judge's desk. Six of the jurors went into the jury room, and six of the jurors went into the other room. The jurors did not use the judge's chamber normally. Law books for the judge and lawyers were located there. Today, other individuals in the room were not part of the case. It was unclear if they had said anything about the case to sway the jury members. That should have presented a problem, but the bailiff was attending to the other jurors, and this issue went unnoticed for the moment.

Both rooms had a toilet for any jury member who needed to use it, but there was not a door between the two rooms. In leaving the courtroom, the jurors tried to leave together. Having to descend the double staircase outside that split going in opposite directions did not seem to be an obstacle that could cause any problems. The group headed to the house just a short distance from the courthouse after going down the right set of stairs. The bailiff went as an overseer to make sure there was no outside influence, and they kept together. One of the other jurors noticed there were only eleven members present while they walked toward their awaiting meal. The juror notified the bailiff, and a court official had to be summoned to stay with the eleven while the lost panel member was located.

Mr. T. J. Shubert had been in the toilet. When he came out, he was alone. He tried to overtake the group and took the left set of steps and got separated from the group. They lost him in the crowds of people standing around talking about what should happen in the case. Some people thought it was self-defense, while some advocated the death penalty for the cold-blooded murderer. As loud as the attendees were talking, the juror could not help but hear most of the conversations in the yard.

Once the group got to the boarding house, they served them cured ham and red-eye gravy with homemade biscuits, leather britches, and boiled potatoes. For dessert, Mrs. Shubert served a sweet potato cobbler and coffee. After eating, the jury left the boarding house.

Everyone thanked her and complimented her on the meal she served. They returned to the courthouse to do what the county had assigned them to do. This trial would not be an easy one.

The twelve members of the panel entered the courtroom and proceeded to the seats reserved for the jury. The bailiff surveyed the room and informed the judge that all parties were ready to begin. Judge Stark enters the courtroom after the bailiff instructs everyone to stand. He takes his seat at the bench and instructs the Clerk of Court to swear in the jury. The Clerk gestured for the jury to stand and faced them and said, "Will the jury please raise your right hand?" Wash thought the pause waiting for them to stand was an eternity. The clerk finally read, "Do you swear to try the case before this court, and that you will return a true verdict according to the evidence and the instructions of the court, so help you, God?" Each member said, "I do?"

The judge read about the case to the jury after the clerk swore them in. He states, "This case is number 254, The State versus Wash Smith for murder. It is in the name and on behalf of the citizens of Georgia, charge and accuses Wash Smith of the County and State aforesaid with the offense of Murder for that the said Wash Smith on 3rd.day of January, in the year of our Lord Nineteen Hundred and Twenty-Eight in the county and State aforesaid, did: unlawfully, and with force and arms, make an assault in and upon one Jud L. Wells in the peace of God and said State being unlawfully, feloniously, willfully and of his malice aforethought, did kill and murder, by shooting the said a Jud L. Wells with a certain shotgun which they said Wash Smith held and giving to the said Jud L. Wells a mortal wound, of which mortal wound the said Jud L. Wells died."

Now that the trial had started, it was time for both lawyers to stand before the court to make an opening statement to the judge and jurors. The dramatics involved in that process, as the lawyers eloquently presented their case, made Wash even more anxious. Wash's thoughts were racing through his mind in hopes things went as he hoped. He knew the situation he was in, and he had visualized the scene back in January too many times to count. That day came and passed, so if it could change things, it would be impossible now. He sat wringing his hands as the proceeding developed and the trial continued.

Mr. Pemberton Cooley, the solicitor general for the State, stood up first and faced the jury and said, "Your Honor and Gentlemen of the jury; the state has charged the defendant with the crime of murdering Jud L. Wells. The State will prove with no doubt that the killing of Jud L. Wells was a felonious murder and that the state should pass judgment to the maximum sentence allowed by the law." Wash knew that the maximum sentence allowed meant death by an electric chair. He wanted to object, but the power of the statement weighed him down. He could not move. His mind raced, his heart pounded, and he fought back emotions. He had to keep thinking that he knew with no doubt it was self-defense.

When the State completed its opening remarks, Wash's lawyer, Mr. Finnley Barrett, stood and faced the jury. He said, "Your Honor and Gentlemen of the jury; under the law, a person may protect themselves from acts of terror. The defense sets out to prove that Wash only reacted in self-defense and that the crime was not that of felonious murder, as the State had said." Wash just knew that his lawyer would speak on his behalf. He could not make himself say or think about that remark being felonious murder.

His lawyer told the judge, "I'm ready to begin the trial."

The lawyers can draw the opening statements out, but the two lawyers kept their statements to a minimum. The sheriff had collected some items during the initial investigation of the crime that had to be presented as evidence. This process took time to present and enter the evidence into the records book for the trial. The sheriff and lawyer identified the gun used during the crime and tagged it along with the shells, both fired and unfired. They listed the pocket knife Jud used. Wash was sure there was a weapon under the counter at the store, but they did not list one as evidence. If there had been one, what happened to it? There had never been a case like this one in Banks County, and the murder had affected too many lives. A mistake Wash must face and one that will not be easy.

The judge looked at the time and thought it best to recess for the afternoon. Questioning another witness now would make the trial go too far into the next hour. He reminded the jury of his instructions earlier and dismissed them till the next day.

At the end of the first day, Wash was glad it was over. His mother was hoping to touch him before he left, and the sheriff did not object to a quick embrace. He nodded goodbye and left with the sheriff to walk back to the jail. He had to put back on his prison clothes to save the suit for tomorrow. The sheriff told Wash just to slip the tie over his head without untying it. In the morning, it will be easier to fix; he told Wash. The black-and-white striped clothes the jail had for him to wear were too big and baggy on him. The suit was new, and he wanted nothing to happen to it that might spoil its looks. He ate very little of the supper provided to him and tried to lie down. Rest was difficult for Wash that night. He stayed up late in his cell by himself, and it was cool and hard to stay warm. At that point, he felt alone with nobody to turn to. It was good to see his mother and grandfather, but there was a lot on his mind and thoughts kept jumping between family and the trial.

The next morning after a restless night, the sheriff woke Wash and brought him a small breakfast of eggs, gravy, and a biscuit. His breakfast reminded him of what his mother had prepared for him at home. The sheriff brought him his suit. He carefully put it on and tucked his shirt neatly into his pants. He did not undo the tie the night before and slipped it back around his neck. After he dressed, he waited in the chair next to the sheriff's desk until it was time to go. When the sheriff told him it was time, Wash stood and placed his hands behind his back for the handcuffs. He did not give the officer any problems with having the cuffs put around his wrists. The two of them talked as they crossed the road to the courthouse on the second day of the trial.

He wondered if his mother would be there today. Wash entered as he did on the first day of the trial and took his chair from before. His mother and grandfather attended and occupied the same two seats as yesterday. He knew this must be a troublesome time for her, but it eased him to see her presence.

The Courthouse Homer, Georgia

CHAPTER 12:
THE PROSECUTION
WITNESS

The judge ordered the State to bring forth its first witness. There were eleven witnesses scheduled on the docket to testify for the State. Wash knew most of the witnesses by name or worked with them. He felt more at ease entering this stage of the trial. Surely, it would become obvious he was not the criminal the State wanted everybody to believe. The first witness to enter the witness stand, after being duly sworn in, was Will Freeman. He wore just his everyday clothes but not his work ones. The first witness took his seat between the judge and the jury and nervously looked around. He did not like the fact that he was the first person called and settled his mind that he would have his part over.

The prosecuting attorney, Mr. Cooley, stood with his binder of questions and asked, "Will you please state your name and tell the court where you live?"

Will could not look toward Wash. He finally raised his head and answered, "My name is Will Freeman, and I live in the upper edge of Banks County in Columbia District."

Mr. Cooley turned toward the witness and asked, "How long had you known Mr. Wells?"

"I knew Mr. Jud L. Wells in his lifetime since he was a boy. He is about forty-three or four. I live about a mile or two from him for about nine years," Will stated.

Mr. Cooley continued interviewing the witness with, "Just how do you know Wash Smith?"

"I know Wash Smith and have known him since he was a kid." Will commented and added, "He's something like twenty, I guess. He lived with Delmar Chitwood, something like a half a mile from Mr. Wells' house. He had been living there a month or maybe longer. He was raised back in the mountains like six or eight miles."

The attorney for the State checked his notes for questions and asked, "When did you first meet up with Mr. Smith that morning?"

Will responded, "I met him about two hundred yards from home hunting Jud, wanting to get in the store. He wanted to get some shells to go hunting, he told me."

The State attorney inquired, "Do you live close to Mr. Wells?"

Will thought for a minute and responded, "I live on Mr. Wells' place about three hundred yards from his house, live there as a tenant. I moved there on Monday before this happened on Tuesday and had lived there before. I have been with him for about nine years."

"Where had you been that morning, and when did you meet Wash?" Cooley pressed.

Will elaborated, "I was something like three hundred yards from Mr. Wells' store or more, to where I met Wash. That was about one or one-thirty. I was going home, and he was going towards Mrs. Smith's where I had been killing hogs. Jud assisted me in killing the hog that morning about dinner time. That was all the conversation that passed between Wash and me."

"When was the next time you saw Wash?" the attorney questioned.

Will thought about what to say and testified. "He came to my house about four o'clock and wanted me to go with him to Jud's store. I told him I didn't have time, and he kept on wanting me to go up there and eat some can goods with him. I was out of tobacco and I told him I would go up there and get some tobacco and I went with him to the store, just me and Wash. It is something like three hundred yards from my house to the store, and there is a road leading from my house to the store. Mr. Wells' store is twenty-five or thirty feet, I expect, from his dwelling house. In going from my house to the store, you reach the store first. When we got up to the place where Mr. Wells lived, he was in the house. It was a snowy day. Neither one of us went into the house. Wash called him Jud, and Mr. Wells came to the door. The store was locked, so we went to Jud's house and called him."

The attorney tried to determine who might have heard anything more, and he expressed, "Who was at the store, and what happened just before the incident? Was it just the three of you?"

Puzzled by his question about three people, Will responded, "No, Wash told him to come down to the store and bring a bowl and two spoons; he wanted some can goods to eat. Mr. Wells came out with the bowl and spoons and went to the store. Oliver Brock was there, and he came out of the house with him. Wash and me just went walking up to the store together, and we all went in the front side by side. Mr. Wells walked up in the yard at the store and opened the door and we went in."

"Was Mr. Smith carrying a gun at the time?" Mr. Cooley insisted.

Will turned his head and looked out the window as if to mentally revisit the scene, "When I first met Wash Smith, he had a double-barrel shotgun, and when he came to my house around four o'clock, he had the same gun and carried that same gun to Mr. Wells' store. On reaching the store, Mr. Wells opened the door and went in. Brock went in the storehouse and so did I. All went in together. Mr. Smith, when he got into the store, set his gun up against the end of the counter. He carried the gun in the store about three and a half or four feet. He carried it in the store by the barrel. I told him to lay it down; it might fall down and kill somebody. I said set that gun down or lay it down. It's liable to fall and kill somebody, and he picked it up and laid it across the end of the counter."

The attorney looked at Will. "What was Mr. Wells doing?"

Will explained his version, "Mr. Wells at the time was behind the counter cutting the can goods. When we got in the store, Wash told Mr. Wells he wanted some tomatoes. Mr. Wells cut a can of tomatoes and poured it in the bowl. He got the tomatoes off the shelf and cut them with his pocket knife. Wash told him, 'these things have got ice in 'em', and Mr. Wells said, 'I will warm them up at the house'. Then Wash wanted some oysters. Mr. Wells reached under the counter and got a can of oysters and was talking to me about killing hogs, he asked me if I salted the old lady's hog down, and then he cut the can of oysters and set them down by the bowl, and then he just shot him in the neck, on the right side of the neck. I didn't look at the wound until the next morning. I just seed him where he was bleeding. I seed the lad hit him, you know. Mr. Smith was about eight feet from Mr. Wells when his gun fired. Mr. Wells was asking me had I went and salted the hog I killed that morning when he was shot."

Mr. Cooley walked closer to the witness and asked, "Where were the others when he shot Mr. Wells?"

Will continued with his testimony, "At that time Mr. Brock was sitting on a sack of bran right on the right of me, about halfway from the door. Mr. Wells was just talking, and he hadn't said anything to make Wash mad that I heard. Wash didn't say anything to Mr. Wells just before he shot him, just asked for the oysters. When the gun fired, I whirled around and looked at him and asked him what he meant. He said he had killed a shepherd dog and was going to kill two more. I ran out the door something like a hundred and fifty yards, I guess. I stopped running and went to walking after I got out of sight of him."

"Did you see Mr. Smith again that day?" Mr. Cooley proposed.

"I didn't see him until about nine o'clock that night. I didn't see him leave the store. This was in Banks County. When I saw Wash Smith about one o'clock that day, he was stomping a brush pile like he was scaring a rabbit out. He had a gun and a dog." Will told the court.

The State interrogated, "Had you or anybody been drinking?"

Will thought for a minute and added, "If he had been drinking, I couldn't tell it. Mr. Brock was sober and Mr. Wells was sober and so was I."

"Did Mr. Wells live alone, and did he have any weapons?" Cooley questioned.

Will knew Jud's sister and told Mr. Cooley, "Mr. Wells was a single man. He and his sister Miss Minnie lived at the Wells' house. She was at home when this happened. At the time Mr. Wells was shot, the only weapon that I seed was a little pocket knife that he was cutting the can with, and he did not cut Mr. Smith with that knife."

"Well, if all he had was a pocket knife, how close was Mr. Wells to Mr. Smith? Was there anything between the two of them?" he asked Will.

Will told the lawyer, "I was seven or eight feet from Mr. Smith when he shot Jud. There was a little counter, something like waist height between them."

"When he shot, what did you do?" Cooley proposed to Will.

Will looked around the courtroom and replied, "There was just one shot fired while I was there and one when I was about fifty or seventy-five yards from the house. Nobody was with me. I looked back and Oliver Brock was leaving the house when the second gunshot coming towards me."

The State's attorney inquired, "Had Mr. Smith bought anything in the store?"

He had to think for a minute to remember if Wash had bought any of the things he wanted before he answered and said, "Wash didn't buy any shells from Mr. Wells; he never paid for anything, for the oysters or tomatoes."

Mr. Cooley remembered he wanted shells and asked Will, "I thought he told you he wanted some shells; did he buy any?"

Will told Cooley, "I went back the next morning and saw the shells that Mr. Wells was shot with. There was two lying there in front of the store where they picked them up. After the gun was fired, he was trying to unbreech it or get the hammer back. I don't know which. The next morning, I saw twelve gauge shells yellow-looking. They had been cut half in two. I don't know what effect that would have on the shells."

The State's lawyer turned and walked to his seat and nodded to Wash's lawyer, showing that he had finished questioning the witness and if he had anything to ask he could. Wash had been anxious the entire time since Will was answering questions. The lawyer did not ask him anything that would have shown it to be self-defense. He asked nothing about what Jud had said. The remark Jud made "Or else!" was still fresh in Wash's memory. That was not anything he could forget so quickly.

Wash's lawyer got up from his seat and proceeded to the witness stand. He said, "Just how well do you know Mr. Wells?"

Will slowly began, "I am forty-eight years old, and I was born and raised between here and Currahee Mountain. I have been where I am now, about nine years, and near there practically all my life, and have been at work for Mr. Wells for seven or eight years. I have been a tenant on his farm and the other boys. I made a crop there last year. I made six bales of cotton. I just had one plow and three hoe hands."

"Who else lived on the farm as tenants?" Mr. Barrett wanted to know.

"Mrs. Smith lived something like a quarter of a mile from Mr. Wells on the old Wells home place," Will continued and said. "Two boys and her girl lived with her. That is where I killed hogs that day. It was a real cold day, and I killed hogs that morning. They sent me up there to get a barrel and I had to get the ice out of it and I didn't get back until about one o'clock."

Wash thought that he had heard most of this earlier and wondered why it was important to repeat just about everything, word for word. He supposed his lawyer had a reason for it and trusted his know-how in the matter.

Mr. Barrett stopped Will and asked, "When did you say that you saw Wash Smith?"

Will hesitated and tried to remember what he had said earlier. He paused and took a deep breath and said, "I saw Wash Smith about one o'clock. I hadn't seen Oliver Brock up to that time. I hadn't seen Dudley Ayers that day, and I hadn't seen Calloway Freeman until that night. Neither had I seen Curtis Smith nor Horace Smith that day. I don't know anything about no still place. I hadn't drank any liquor at all that day. I don't drink any liquor at all. I hadn't been running any stills there. It was one or one-thirty when I first met Smith and he was going towards Mrs. Smith's. He asked me was Jud down there. It was about one or half-past one when I found Wash hunting. He went on towards Mrs. Smith's and I went home. I don't know what became of Wash Smith from that time until four o'clock. I was at home and he came by there."

The defense lawyer asked, "When did Wash see Mr. Wells earlier, and was anybody with him?"

Will rubbed his forehead and responded, "I think he saw Wells over at Mrs. Smith's. That's what they told me. I didn't see him. Wells went in the store first. Wells was in the house warming when me and him went up to the house and called him out and we went on up to the store, me and Wash went to the store together. Mr. Brock come out of the house with Mr. Wells."

Mr. Barrett thought that the men may have been drinking moonshine during the day and asked, "Was anybody drinking?"

"Nobody was drinking as I could tell. I hadn't seen Wash drink any that day." Will responded.

As the lawyer walked over to his table, he turned and asked, "What happened when you got to the store?"

Will replied, "When we got to the store, we stood in the yard just long enough to call Mr. Wells and for him to walk about twenty or twenty-five feet. The store door was locked. We were all just standing there in the yard, and I wouldn't say which one went in first. There is a little platform out in front of the store about five feet wide. It likes about an inch or half an inch being as high as the floor, just room enough for a little plank to be laid upon it."

The lawyer had to keep stopping him from going on. He asked Will, "Was anybody mad?"

Will slowly lowered his head to remember what had happened and replied, "Nobody was mad. Mr. Wells was just laughing and talking. Everything was peaceful and nobody was mad."

The defense attorney thought that once they entered the store, something had brought about a change in attitude and asked Will, "The store is small and surely you heard something said?"

Will answered, "When I went in the store, I went straight by the side of the counter. Mr. Brock was on the right, sitting on a sack of bran. The counter come up about a third of the side, and I was about halfway between the door and where the counter made its turn. I was standing on the side of the counter, and when the gunshot, it shot across my head and shoulder. At that time, Mr. Brock was at my right. Mr. Wells was at the back of the house, facing the door. The counter runs around on the left-hand side and to the back. I was talking to Wells."

"Did you talk about whiskey?" pleaded Mr. Barrett.

Will thought about how he should answer the question and finally said, "No whiskey was mentioned. Wash Smith's front foot was inside the door and his back foot was where the door facing us. We hadn't been in there, over five minutes, not that long when the shooting occurred."

Mr. Barrett raised his hand and asked, "What were you talking to Mr. Wells about?"

"I was talking to Mr. Wells about the hog we had killed that morning," Will stated.

Wash's lawyer added, "What did Mr. Smith say to Mr. Wells once they got in the store?"

Will waited before he spoke and wanted to make sure he could speak before he continued. Will said, "Wash didn't say anything to Mr. Wells about anything except the tomatoes and oysters. Wash Smith's gun was lying on the end of the counter near the door, and I told him to pick it up; it was liable to fall over and kill somebody, and he took it up and laid it down on the end of the counter. I was facing Mr. Wells, and Mr. Brock was just sitting there. I wouldn't say which way he was looking. Mr. Brock was in reaching distance from me and could have put his hands on me. There was no disagreement or fuss of any kind between any of us. Wash was behind me and raised his gun to shoot over my shoulder. I was sort of leaning against the counter."

The defense thought Mr. Wells would have been more vigilant about what was going on and asked Will, "Did Mr. Wells defend himself?"

Will was not sure what he meant and said, "Mr. Wells liked about five inches being as tall as I am, and he weighed about one hundred and forty-five or fifty pounds. I guess. Wash Smith is five and a half. Wash called Mr. Wells to the store. I told Morgan Evans the same thing about this case that I have sworn today. I was as thoroughly and completely at myself that day as I am now. I have talked to a good many people about this case."

Mr. Cooley stopped Will and asked, "Who is Mr. Evans?"

Will explained, "Mr. Evans lived four or five miles back towards Baldwin from where I live. Some call Mrs. Smith Sue Smith and some call her Sue Brady. She and her boys and a little girl, about four or five kids, live together. Her girl's name is Daisy."

Mr. Barrett stopped Will from speaking and thought what he was saying had nothing to do with his point. He needed to redirect him back to more important testimony and found it hard to keep Will on the questions. He rephrased a question, "What did you do when you heard the shot?"

Will remembered how scared he was when Wash shot the gun. He told the lawyer, "When the shot was fired, I run out the door as quick as I could get by the gun and run around the shop out in the road, and I was about fifty yards away when I heard the next shot. I don't mean to say that Mr. Wells didn't own a gun, but there wasn't anything but a knife in the store; that is all I saw. I didn't see any gun. I saw a gun lying up on the table at his home where he slept at night. Wash didn't eat any of the can goods. I didn't see Calloway Freeman and Horace Smith until that night. Horace had gone to town. I saw Curtis Smith about one when I left the house and didn't see him anymore until that night."

Mr. Barrett told the judge he had no more questions for this witness, and the judge told Will he could step down. Will left the courtroom and knew he had to stay in the area in case he had to answer any more questions. Wash tried to grasp why Will was telling it like this. He seemed to ramble on about what he was telling, but just thought he must be nervous and told what he could remember. Surely, one of the other witnesses would support his self-defense. The tension in the courtroom was increasing, and Wash could feel it pressing on him like a weighted blanket. If the witnesses continued like this, he thought he had no hope at all. He knew Oliver came up next to testify. Surely, he will support Wash.

Questioning the first witness took most of the morning, and the next person on the docket would push the time to recess too late in the afternoon. The judge asked the solicitor general if the next witness would be quick to present. Mr. Cooley said it would be rather lengthy and would probably be better to call him after the noon recess. Now would be a time to stop for lunch.

The judge called for a recess of one hour for lunch. The boarding house brought sandwiches in for the jury members to eat in the back room of the courthouse. As many people as there were attending the trial, it was best to avoid the disaster that presented itself the day before. None of the jurors objected to having to stay. They wanted no more issues like what happened with the juror getting lost in the crowd again.

After lunch, the judge took his place at the bench and instructed the State to present its next witness. The witness entered, and the interview continued. Oliver Brock had been waiting outside the main courtroom, and the bailiff went to the door to have him come in. He entered the room and walked toward the witness stand. Not once did Oliver turn to glance in Wash's direction. He could not make eye contact at all. Wash thought that it would be strange for Oliver not to acknowledge him, and he expected the lawyer for the State asked some of the same questions to Oliver after being duly sworn in as a witness for the State that he asked Will. Wash could hear him clearly say, "So help me, God." He lowered his hand and took a seat as the next witness. He sat quietly as he watched the attorney for the State approach him.

The State's lawyer asked, "Where do you live and what were you doing on January 3, 1928?"

Oliver paused for a minute and said, "I live up on Currahee Mountain about two miles above Jud Wells. On January 3, 1928, I was at Jud Wells'. I went down there about one or two o'clock in the evening. Nobody was there except Jud and me. He was at home when I got there. I think he had been down to Mr. Smith's, and he was coming up to his house. I was there for about two hours."

Wash could not follow along with every word that was being said because he was trying to piece together what Oliver and Will had said so far about what he remembered. That day already was a nightmare, and he was relating the two versions he hears to his experience of that fateful day. He keeps hearing the words spoken but in association with what Wash remembers. He recollects many events as the same and some are not what he remembers from his friends.

The State's attorney asks, "When did you first meet Wash and what were you doing?"

Oliver told him, "Wash and Will Freeman came there to Mr. Wells's home while I was there; Mr. Wells and me was in the house when they came."

"Did he say anything to Mr. Wells?" Mr. Cooley asks.

"Wash called Mr. Wells and told him to bring a dish and two spoons if he wanted something to eat. He gets the dish and spoons and went out there to the store.

Mr. Wells went up and unlocked the door, and we all went in." Oliver recalls.

The attorney added, "Was anything going on once inside the store?"

Oliver said, "Wash had a gun on the outside there. Mr. Smith told Mr. Wells he wanted some tomatoes, and Mr. Wells got them and went to cutting them. Wash said something about them being froze and said he wanted some oysters, so Jud reached down and got a can of oysters and put them on the table. Jud turned around and ask Will about salting a hog. The next thing I knowed the gun fired. Wash fired the gun, and it hit Mr. Wells in the neck. I think he fell. Will went out the door, and Wash went behind the counter and throwed the gun down on him, and I turned my head as the gun fired again. Then I run and went on out with Will out to his house."

"Had there been any arguing at any time in the store?" the lawyer for the state asked?

Oliver replied, "Mr. Wells and me was sober and I reckon Wash and Will was sober. I didn't see Mr. Wells do anything to cause Wash Smith to shoot him the first time and didn't hear him say anything to make him mad. Mr. Wells only had a pocket knife in his hand, cutting the tomatoes with it when Smith shot him. He fell on a box behind the counter. I didn't hear him say anything. That was about four o'clock I reckon."

Wash did not think things were going well for him, but he determined that justice would show he acted as he should. The lawyer seemed satisfied so far with how his first two witnesses were doing and he inquired, "Did you see Wash Smith any time after that?"

Oliver thought and said, "I went back there and Wash wasn't out there, but he come back in a little bit and I run as I was afraid he would shoot me. He had the gun. There were several at the store; his sister Miss Minnie was there. When he come back, they went down through the field there. When I got started away from there, I heard the gun shoot two times. I didn't go back to the house until that night after the sheriff got there. I went back up there then."

The State's lawyer said, "No more questions," and turned to face the other table. The lawyer strolled back to his seat in the courtroom as though he had the case locked up in the State's favor. It would be a straightforward case from here on out, and they would lock Wash up to get the punishment he deserved. Wash did not have those same feelings. He hoped the trial would determine the truth to come out as self-defense and let his lawyers and justice prevail.

Wash's lawyer, Mr. Barrett, stood and walked over to the witness stand. He proceeded with the same type of questions he had for Will. Oliver and Wash were about the same age and surely, he would see things the same way Wash did. Mr. Barrett asked Oliver, "Where were you on this morning of January 3, 1928, and who were you with at the time?"

Oliver had never been in a courtroom to be a witness to anyone, and the experience was taking a toll on his mind, so he had to consider his remarks. He said, "I had been home all the morning before going to Mr. Wells' that afternoon. I didn't see Will Freeman that day until he came there with Wash. Before I went to Mr. Wells, I don't think I had seen Horace Smith, Calloway Freeman nor Curtis Smith. Dudley Ayers come on down the road with me, and he went on down to Delmar Chitwood's. I hadn't been at a still drinking that day."

The defense lawyer asked Oliver, "What did you do when you got into the store?"

Oliver sat back in his seat and answered, "He stopped in front of the store before we went in, and Mr. Wells unlocked the door and went in first, and I don't remember who went in next. I was the last one that went in the store. Wash Smith's gun was there at the door somewhere. I never paid much attention; Will asked him something about if it was loaded. It was somewhere about the door at the counter. I was on the left of the store, and I crossed over. Will was setting up on the counter, and I was on the left-hand side and I crossed over and got on the right side. I was on the inside of the store. Will and I were pretty close together. Mr. Wells was in the back of the store about three, four, or five feet from the door. Wash was standing pretty close to the counter."

"Was there a reason for Wash to be at the counter, and what did he do?" Mr. Barrett wondered.

Oliver told him, "I was looking toward Wash and saw him when he raised the gun to fire. There was nothing between he and Mr. Wells when Wash shot Mr. Wells. He walked around the counter. The counter stood about two feet from the door on the left-hand side, and between the front wall of the house and the counter, there was a little space of two or three feet and you walk in between that space to get behind the counter. Wash went to the corner of the counter before he fired. He walked all down behind the counter to the corner of the counter. He was within two or three feet of Mr. Wells. Before the shot was fired, he went behind the counter to the left-hand side and walked down to the corner and then turned back towards Mr. Wells."

Wash's lawyer asked him, "What did you do when you heard the shot? So nobody was angry?"

Thinking about what had happened shook Oliver up, remembering the shooting, and he told the court, "Whenever Wash went behind the counter, I went on to the door. Nothing was said between me and Wash after Wells was shot, and nothing was said between Will and Wash. When I went out the front door after the shooting, both of us turned to the left and went towards Will's. He was ahead of me, a right smart piece. I was right about the door on the outside of the door when the second shot was fired. Will had got to the road. The gun had been fired twice. I run because I didn't know but what he might shoot me. Will started to run before I did."

Mr. Barrett asked his next question. "Did you see Mr. Smith after that?"

Oliver said, "I didn't see Wash when he came out of the store."

"Could you tell if they were mad?" he asked Oliver.

"If Wash was mad at Mr. Wells, I didn't know it. The first thing I knew about anything wrong was when I saw the shot. I saw him raise the gun. At that time, there were no words between Mr. Wells and Wash and there had been no cussing, and I could see nothing to indicate any madness. I don't know why Wash shot Mr. Wells." Oliver clarified for the defense.

Mr. Barrett was trying to follow the sequence of events for the jury's sake and asked Oliver, "Where did you go after he was shot?"

He explained to Mr. Barrett, "After Mr. Wells was shot, I went on out to Mr. Freemans and stayed a little while and then went back out to Mr. Wells in about an hour."

Interrupting Oliver, the lawyer said, "When you returned, what was going on at the store?"

Oliver continued, "There were several people out there when I went back. I went back because when I left there wasn't nobody there but Miss Wells. About half an hour after the shooting, I saw Wash come out the road toward my house that was about four-thirty or five o'clock. After that, I went over to Mr. Davis. Up to the time of the shooting and at the time of the shooting nor during that day, I didn't seen any liquor or didn't see anybody drinking any liquor. So far as I know, Mr. Wells and Mr. Wash Smith were the very best friends. Wash Smith had been around there with Delmar Chitwood about a month or two. I don't know what kind of work he was doing. I hadn't seen him doing any work for the month or two he had been there."

The defense lawyer turned and told the court he had no more questions for this witness, and the judge told Oliver he may step down. The experience shook Oliver and trudged out of the courtroom. Oliver's testimony hurt Wash.

He frequently turned to look at his mother, and every time he did, her eyes were on him. It was as though she knew when he looked her way. His mother wore a church dress to the trial today. Not having a lot of dresses to wear and working on the farm, she only had a few delicate dresses. There was a dress she wore to town, a dress for church, and one dress for funerals. It was whatever was clean. During the day, she wore her older dresses that were stained from cooking or jelly making. She always tied an apron around her thin waist with any dress to protect them from any more stains.

It was near five in the afternoon on the second day of the trial, and the judge called for a recess until the next morning. Wash did not have to be on the witness stand at all that day and sat hour after hour listening to the testimony presented. He had hoped for a better day than the last. It squelched his hopes after each friend stepped down. The court had two witnesses that took some time to complete, and with it being close to five o'clock, it would go into the next hour to call another witness. The judge called for a recess till morning.

Everything ended on the second day, and Wash and the sheriff returned to the jail. The sheriff was trusting Wash a little more. He still kept all the precautions when handling a prisoner by following all the routine procedures. Wash did not say a single word on their way back to the jail. He had a lot on his mind about the proceedings today. All his friends and people he worked with were in court today. It was the first time he had seen most of them since his arrest.

He changed clothes and sat on the edge of his bed, thinking about what he and his friends would do back home. Wash thought about how they would go hunting even though he was much younger than most of them, and they would let him tag along when they went hunting for rabbits or squirrels or fishing in the rivers close to the farm. He remembered when he shot a rabbit and took the trophy home to his mother. She would proudly take the prize and cook it just the way he liked it. She would carefully prepare the meat for a stew. His mother knew he would take pleasure in knowing he helped feed the family and would always let Wash know just how proud she was.

His thoughts always quickly came back to his present situation and finally fell asleep from worry on his bed. The sheriff came with food that evening and saw he was sleeping and just left the plate at the door of the cell. He thought, that when he woke up, he would be hungry and could get it then.

The next morning, when the sheriff went to wake him for the third day of trial, he noticed Wash had not touched the food from the day before. He gave Wash the suit and took the uneaten food away. When Wash changed, he told the sheriff he was ready to go back. He ate very little of the breakfast, and they left for the courtroom.

The bailiff called the third day of the court to order, just as it was all the days before. He called Floyd Holbrooks to the stand, and he stood and approached the witness stand. The bailiff swore in Floyd. He lowered his hand and took his seat. The State's lawyer questioned him about his connection to the case.

The lawyer said, "What work do you do and what can you add to the case concerning Jud L. Wells."

The witness said, "I am in the undertaking business at Cornelia, Georgia. I buried the body of Mr. Jud Wells and prepared the body for burial. I found one wound in the throat and one in the head. The wound in the throat was possibly bigger than a dollar; nearly all the throat was torn out. The other wound was in the back of the head; all the back of the head was torn off. I found the body in a little store down there. It was in kind of a posture back behind the counter on the floor. His face was lying up, I believe."

The State attorney added, "What did you do with the body?"

Mr. Holbrooks said, "I removed the body to the home and embalmed it. The next morning, I removed it to my morgue in Cornelia, and I interred it at Level Grove Cemetery. I buried the body; Mr. Wells was dead when I found him."

"Do you know what was used to kill Mr. Wells?" the lawyer asked.

The witness added, "I presume from the size of the wounds they couldn't have been made with a pistol. I am not definite as to what kind of an instrument it was made with."

The lawyer thanked Mr. Holbrooks for his witness and time and said he had no more questions. The judge instructed the defense if he had any questions. Mr. Barrett shook his head no. The witness left the stand and respectfully left the building. The testimony brought back the scene from the store to Wash. He could see what had happened in his mind and bowed his head in his hands.

The judge checked who was on the list to be called next. He addressed the bailiff to call P. C. Wilbanks. He stood from the last row of seats in the courtroom when the bailiff called his name and approached the Judge. The bailiff swore in Mr. Wilbanks, and the State's attorney asked, "What is your job and what were you doing on January the third?"

The sheriff wore his uniform to the trial and responded, "On January third, I was Sheriff of Habersham County. I recall the death of Mr. Jud Wells. Hr. Hill, my deputy, and several more were something like four or five feet away when we arrested Wash Smith. We went over to a place to make a search for him and was coming on back to the place where Mr. Wells was killed and was coming down the road. I think there were six or seven of us in the bunch. I wouldn't say for certain and were kinder, coming around a big cut around a hill. There was about two in front of me, and I was back about two steps, well those in front heard something. Someone coming up the road, and they kinda stopped and come running back."

"I just dropped on the side of the bank and just sat right down against the side of the bank and had my gun leaning over on this arm, when he come up about even with us. I didn't know who the party was, he was something like the distance from here to that stove say from us and all at once he throwed his gun right that way and as he throwed it up, he cocked both barrels and he said boys I ain't got a damn word to say if you got anything to say it now. Well, I knew I was sitting right there and I couldn't do nothing and he kept his eyes right on me and of course. I was watching to get my chance at him. I thought if I could get his attention off of me I could make two leaps and grab him without shooting him and so about that time Mr. Hill said drop that gun and when he said drop that gun he just wheeled and throwed it on him just that way and two shots fired and I throwed my gun on him and shot as quick as I could and after I shot jumped up and started towards him and pulled my trigger again and my gun wouldn't revolve and he kinda turned around and started to run and I went after him and he throwed his gun down on the ground and so I taken down the road after him and was pretty close to him and my gun wouldn't fire and I thought I would hit him the back of the head and knock him down and I pulled back and throwed the gun at him and I didn't hit him and he run down the road and taken out a ridge road and got away from us. We caught him about something like I guess between two and two-and-a-half hours after that. I knew Mr. Smith, and I had known him, something like two years, I guess. Mr. Smith knew me also."

Mr. Cooley asked, "Where were you, and what time was it when you found the defendant?"

The sheriff from Habersham said, "It was something like around ten o'clock, maybe between nine and ten o'clock that night when we met Mr. Smith. I guess it was about two miles from where this happened. He wasn't asleep when we found him. His arm was broken; he was shot in the arm, and he said he had two shots through his other arm and there was one shot through there. He was at Mr. Brown's when we got him."

"I don't know where he lived; Mr. Whelchel was with me at the time. He is the Sheriff of this county. This is the gun Mr. Smith had that night up there. He shot one of those shells that night there, and that other shell was in the gun when we picked it up. I got the gun about ten or fifteen steps from where the shooting was done. The discharged shell was in the gun. He shot once and one hadn't been shot."

The attorney for the State told Mr. Whelchel that was all he had. The defense promptly said he had no questions, and the sheriff left the court. Judge Stark asked for the State to bring the next witness that was on the docket. The bailiff called for the sheriff of Banks County, S. J. Whelchel. Once the state duly swore in Mr. Whelchel as a witness, he took his seat on the witness stand.

Wash did not know how the sheriff would help his case, but could not see how it would hurt it either. The attorney for the State stood and approached the sheriff and proceeded with his first question. The attorney said, "Sheriff, can you tell me what happened when you came upon the scene of the crime back in January?"

Sheriff Whelchel said, "Sheriff Wilbanks turned that gun over to me the night the shooting occurred up there. He turned this cartridge and this shell over to me, and the other one was picked up there at the store. I have had them down in the vault in the Clerk's office. The night Mr. Smith was arrested, he had five or six shells, but there wasn't any of them out like that one."

"He had a pocketknife and five dollars and twenty cents in pennies, and nickels and dimes, and one fifty-cent piece and a ten-dollar bill up here in his pocket. The officers shot five, six, seven, or eight times. I don't know who did the shooting. I was not close by. It was about two miles from the point where the shooting occurred to the point where Wash was found and about three or four hours later. He was shot in here and in here and in here and his arm was broken both bones. He was in bed when we found him. He didn't try to run. I pulled the cover back off of him, and I don't know whether he knowed me or not, but he told me not to be so rough."

Sheriff Whelchel almost knew that the defense attorney would not be asking him questions. He started to stand once he answered the question but thought it best to wait for the judge to dismiss him from the stand. The State's lawyer said that would be all. The judge looked toward the defense lawyer, and he shook his head to show he had no questions for this witness.

The bailiff called for Felton Presley to come forward to be sworn in. He raised his hand like all the others and swore to tell the whole truth and nothing but the truth. He lowered his right hand and had a seat. The State attorney asked, "How did you get the package of shells?"

Felton stated, "Mr. Wiley Brown gave me that package the next morning after Wells was killed, and it has been at my house ever since."

The bailiff told Felton Presley that he could step down and called Wiley Brown to the stand.

Felton's testimony confused Wash, and he wondered why it was important to know that. He passed it off as unnecessary testimony. Wash thought it was of no help to him and did not see how it could help the State. He saw Wiley entering the courtroom and knew his testimony might clear up his confusion. The state swore in Wiley, and he took his seat near the judge. Every once in a while Wash looked at the jury to see if he could decide what would be their decision. He listened carefully to every word Wiley spoke.

The lawyer for the State checked over his notes at the table before he stood and proceeded with his questioning. He needed to read over the summary about the purpose of this witness before he could begin. The pause, he hoped, would settle the nervousness the witness was having. He slowly walked to Wiley and smiled. He said, "How do you know Mr. Smith, and what do you have to say about the evidence that has been brought before this court?"

Wiley began, "My name is Wiley Brown. Wash Smith laid them shells on the table at my house. They are the ones. He had twelve shells. Two of them was buckshot and one was cut and one red one was cut. He laid them down on the table at my house when he started to bed about twelve o'clock."

The prosecuting attorney asked, "What were you doing when Mr. Smith came to your house and what did he want?"

Wiley answered saying, "He come in the house and I was lying on the bed, and he said I better do something about my arm and I said what's the matter with it and he said it's shot up and I said how come and he said he killed Jud Wells and the law done it and I asked him four or five times about it and he said if I didn't believe it I could go up there and I would see them damn brains in his hat. This was between twelve and two o'clock before he went to sleep. He come up and hollowed for me and come on in and sent me for a doctor."

The lawyer asked again about the shells, "What was unusual about the shells? Were they shot?"

Wiley said, "I broke one yellow shell. I gave them to Felton. I took a handful of the shells and a gun and took them with me after the doctor. I thought I had better take it. I didn't get all of them off the table. I got one good buckshot shell. I took a shot out of that one and he had one of these. I broke it into one good buckshot shell and one piece. I give them to Presley because he asked me for them. I offered them to Gus Wells, and he said give them to Presley. I don't reckon any of the shells had been fired that are out. I could tell if they had been shot. They had gunpowder in them, I reckon. That one had. These had powder but no shot. The shot in it ain't took out. I suppose they had gunshot in them. There is no cap and powder there. The red one had no powder and no cap."

Wiley thought for a minute and continued, "These four will fit the same gun. The only difference is the color of them. These are the shells that he put on the table when he come here. Three of them is; that's all I got there that I ever seed. I didn't get all of them off the table. I never give him no good one like that at all. That was on the morning after the killing."

The State's lawyer said,"No more questions."

The defense had no questions either. The judge told the witness he could stand and leave. Wash at this point was sitting there waiting for all this to pass. He thought that so far today the testimony was more of just a fact and not about it being self-defense.

Daisy walked through the door. Wash was so glad to see her and was sure this would clear up the situation. He felt sure she would support his defense. She raised her hand and swore to tell the truth.

Mr. Cooley approached Daisy and nodded to her with a smile. He could tell by the look on her face that the stress was more than she had ever faced before. She sat at the witness stand, twisting the ring on her finger. He said, "Can you please give this court your name?"

Fidgeting and with a shaky voice, she answered, "My name is Daisy Smith Burns. I have not heard any of the evidence in this case. I have been downstairs all the time." She spoke softly and said, "I have been married about two months to Milton Burns."

She paused, and with her head lowered, Mr. Cooley told her to relax. He waited till she felt more at ease and said, "How do you know Mr. Smith and Mr. Wells?"

She spoke softly and said, "I know Wash Smith and have known him for a good while. I am sixteen years old. I knew Mr. Jud Wells during his lifetime and have known him all my life. I did not tell Wash Smith that Mr. Jud Wells had made improper proposals to me at any time, as Mr. Wells had not done so. I went with Wash Smith two times in all. There was no engagement of marriage between Wash Smith and me." She paused in the middle of what she was going to say and hoped she didn't sound like she was rambling around with the answer. She continued, "I live at present at Commerce. My mother lives in Banks County on the Wells place. We have lived there ten years. I was practically raised there. We lived three or four hundred yards from the Wells house. Mr. Wells was down at our house that morning. He come down there and in passing would stop by. Wash Smith, occasionally, stopped at our house. I went out with him just two times."

The States' attorney stopped her thinking she had gotten off the question and asked, "So do you still live at the Wells' place?"

Daisy looked around to get her thoughts together. She said, "I got up here this morning about nine o'clock. I came from Commerce with Charles Craig. He lives at Commerce also. I had a subpoena to come. I think sheriff Whelchel's boy brought it to me last night. Mr. Craig is a taxi driver. I don't know who hired the taxi. I didn't. We didn't have to pay anything for the car. Mr. Craig is no kin to me. We live in the house with him, and he was coming over here, and I came with him."

Mr. Cooley turned to the judge and said, "I have no more questions for this witness." Then, without another remark, went to sit. Wash's attorney stood and told the court he only had one question for the witness.

The defense attorney stood, approached Daisy, and did not want to pressure her unnecessarily. He asked, "Did you ever tell Wash Smith that Mr. Wells was going to harm him in any way?"

Daisy despondently answered, "I did not ever tell Wash Smith that Mr. Jud Wells said he was going to kill him. Mr. Wells never talked to me about Smith at all and Mr. Smith never spoke to me about Mr. Wells."

The defense walked away and signaled to the judge he had no more questions for Mrs. Burns. She did not immediately get up, thinking more questions would come, since she had never been in a courtroom before and was not sure what to do. The judge calmly told her she could step down and leave if she had no more to add to her statement. Standing slowly, she placed her purse on her arm and proceeded out of the courtroom.

The next witness was the person with whom Wash was living. He, like all the others, lived close to each other. The bailiff called Mr. Chitwood to the stand. He raised his hand and swore to tell the truth. The State's attorney approached Delmar and presented the question, "What is your name, and how do you know the two mentioned in this case?"

Delmar nodded and testified, "My name is Delmar Chitwood. I know Wash Smith and have known him for a year or two. I knew Mr. Jud Wells in his lifetime. Wash Smith worked for me. I don't know whether he was working for me or not on or about January 3, 1928. He was with me through Christmas. I don't know whether he worked for me in January some or not. He was staying at my house when he killed Jud Wells."

Mr. Cooley wondered why he was staying at his house and asked, "Why was Mr. Smith staying at your house?"

Mr. Chitwood looked up toward the ceiling as if to be thinking and told the court, "He hired to me to make a crop for 1928. He had been staying at my house maybe two months. I don't know exactly when we made the trade to make the crop this year, but it was before Christmas."

The State lawyer questioned him, "Is there other work you and Mr. Smith do other than farming?"

Delmar acted nervously and looked around to see if some of the other witnesses were in the courtroom. He answered cautiously, "Horace Smith, Calloway Freeman, and Wash Smith, and me did not make any liquor anywhere during that time. I don't know anything about Jud Wells making liquor up there. I don't know anything about his business. I don't know anything about Wash Smith being hired to Wells to make liquor."

The lawyer for the state expressed to Mr. Barrett that he had no more questions. The judge saw him letting the defense attorney know and told the lawyer to question him. Mr. Barrett said, "No questions at the moment." At that point, Delmar Chitwood stood and left as quickly as he entered.

Wash thought he made no comment that helped him in the case. However, making the statement that Wash killed Mr. Wells was damaging enough.

As Delmar was leaving the courtroom, Horace Smith was entering. The two of them nodded but did not speak. Horace heard Judge Stark call his name to come to be sworn in. He raised his hand like all the others and said, "I do."

The attorney for the State said, "State your name and how you know Mr. Smith and Mr. Wells?"

Horace slid back to get comfortable in the witness stand and said, "My name is Horace Smith; I know Wash Smith and I also knew Jud Wells during his lifetime."

Mr. Cooley added, "Do you work for Mr. Wells to make moonshine?"

Shaking his head he said, "Wash Smith, Calloway Freeman, Ayers, and me were not employed by Mr. Jud Wells to manufacture liquor at any time."

"Where were you on January 3rd, 1928?" Cooley spoke.

Horace considered his answer and replied, "The day Mr. Jud Wells was killed, I was gone to Baldwin. I stayed there practically all day. Calloway Freeman was with me. They told me about it just as we were getting home. That was after the killing. My mother's name is Sue Smith. I went to Baldwin that day to get my mother some medicine, but I didn't get it. I stayed there nearly all day."

So, the State wanted to clear up his testimony and asked Horace, "Do you live on the farm owned by Mr. Wells and work for him to make moonshine?"

Horace took a deep breath and paused. He said, "If I was employed to make liquor, I wouldn't care a bit for telling it, and if I was making it, I would tell it. I have never made any liquor and have never helped make any, and I was not employed by anybody to make any liquor. I guess I could tell what liquor was. I have been living on the Wells place eleven years. I don't know of any work that Wash Smith did there for Mr. Wells as being hired by him. If Wash Smith was hired by Mr. Wells to make liquor, I didn't know it."

The State's attorney went to the table and sat down. Mr. Barrett shook his head when the judge asked if he wanted to question this witness. The defense attorney thought Horace would add more to the case since he was at a distance from the farm on the day of the shooting. Horace looked relieved and left.

There was only one more witness the plaintiff had on the agenda to witness. It was Calloway Freeman. As with all the other witnesses, the State asked the same question to start the interviewing. He asked him, "Tell the court your name, and how do you know the victim and the defendant."

Calloway answered, "My name is Calloway Freeman. I am the son of Will Freeman. I knew Jud Wells in his lifetime. I know Wash Smith also."

Mr. Cooley asked Calloway, "Do you work on the farm with Jud Wells to distill liquor?"

"I was not employed by Mr. Wells to make liquor with these other boys," Calloway argued.

"Where were you on the third of January 1928?" the State's lawyer questioned.

Calloway Freeman knew Horace had testified earlier and wanted to make sure he was correct in what he was about to say. Calloway said, "I had gone to Baldwin the day Mr. Wells was killed. I went with Horace Smith to get some medicine for his mother. We found out Mr. Wells was dead that evening when we got back from town. We went to town that morning at about eight or nine o'clock and got back between four and five. We got the medicine for his mother and brought it home and gave it to her."

The State asked him, "Is there anything you want to say that is important to this case?"

The young Mr. Freeman added, "I don't know anything about those two stills. I never saw a still in my life, and if I had, I don't guess I would tell on anybody."

The attorney for the defense said he could step down that he had no questions for this witness. Wash thought that it had been a long day, and all the testimony present that day exhausted him. Not a single witness backed Wash's statement up about it being self-defense. He could not understand why the witness that could back him up did not come to defend his statement. There were still too many unanswered questions that had to be presented on Wash's behalf to show that he defended himself.

After the day's interviews with the witnesses on the trial, Wash felt like everybody he knew had betrayed him. He could not understand why people he thought were close to him were suddenly so distant. The person he lived with, the people he worked with, and the person he loved had all turned their backs to him at a time he needed them the most.

The judge inquired if there were any more witnesses for the State. Mr. Cooley stood and told the judge that he had no more questions. All the witnesses had been cross-examined and the defense could present their witnesses. The only person left to question would be Wash in his own defense. Judge Stark called for a recess to be an hour for lunch.

The jury wanted to stay in the courthouse for lunch as they did on Tuesday. All members felt that staying close to the chamber was easier than leaving the building. They sat quietly and ate what the county provided for them. Like on Tuesday, the boarding house in town sent a small meal to be passed out among the members of the jury. The hour gave them long enough time to prepare for the rest of the trial.

Courtroom Homer, Georgia

CHAPTER 13:
THE DEFENSE WITNESS

After the hour, the jury returned to the courtroom. Prepared to finish the day and hopefully go home to their loved ones, the jury sat solemnly, waiting for the last witness to enter the witness stand. The bailiff called for Wash Smith to please stand and come to the front of the courtroom. Wash calmly stood at the chair he had been sitting in for several days, and the sheriff took the handcuffs off, then patted him on the shoulder. He gently walked to the witness to be interviewed. As he was walking to the front of the courtroom, he glanced back at his mother, and she pressed her lips together and bowed her head. She closed her eyes to show that she loved him.

She could not help but think about his life as she saw her son walk to the witness stand. She could not help but think back on some of those stories and wonder just how this tragic event happened to just a young boy in the early stages of his life. His mother remembered stories about a young Wash and how he loved the outdoors; memories of Wash's childhood came flowing back into his mother's mind. He said to her, "Mama, I bet you can't find me." She remembered Wash enjoying hiding from her around the house when the weather would not let him go outside. His mother hunted for him, pretending not to know where he had hidden. She never let him know she could see him or hear him under the bed or behind a door. Even at an early age, he knew she did her best to take care of the family. It was the same with every family in and around the community. And it was with great care Wash did what he could to help. Oh, how she longed for those days again.

The white handkerchief she had been carrying during the trial caught the tears that streamed down her face. Her heart pounded from fear for her son, and she prayed for him to have courage. She wrung her hands the entire time he was on the stand, folding and unfolding her handkerchief. He sat down in the chair and waited for the State's attorney to question him about what happened. Mr. Cooley stood and slowly approached Wash. Wash could not slow down his heart from pounding in his chest. He tried to relax, folded his arms in his lap, and waited. The wait, he thought, was eternal, but only seconds had passed.

Mr. Cooley asked Wash, "What was going on in your life to take such a drastic motive that happened on Tuesday, January 3rd, 1928?"

Wash took his time to answer. He thought about how to put his words together so everyone would know why. He began, "Well, about two months before this happened, I hired to Mr. Wells to work by the day. Well, he taken me and Mr. Freeman, a man by the name of Freeman, and a man named Brock and Ayers, and had us operating one of these distilleries. Well, at the same time he was running another distillery with Horace Smith and Curtis Smith and Calloway Freeman, Mr. Freeman's son operating the other one. There was two distilleries we were operating for Mr. Wells."

Wash paused, and the attorney asked, "How long had you known Mr. Wells?"

"I had known him all my life, and I knowed he had been having whiskey made and this was the first time I ever worked for him." Wash continued and paused again.

"If you had known him that long, what would have been your motive to take his life?" the attorney pressured Wash.

Wash tried to explain and said, "He had a family there on this place, a woman named Smith. She had several children, and some folks said that some of her children belonged to Jud Wells. She had one daughter about sixteen years old named Daisy, which I had been going to see; for the last year I had been going to see this girl, and the girl was a good girl so far as I know, and I loved the girl and would have married the girl if this trouble hadn't happened." Wash stopped to get his thoughts together.

Mr. Cooley interrupted Wash and said, "That doesn't tell me why, but Mr. Wells tried to take care of the people living on his land?"

Wash tried to tell him how he felt and told Mr. Cooley, "But sometime several weeks before this Jud had seemed to be mad with me, whenever going to the distillery, or back from the distillery, going back and forward, but we worked on and I didn't say anything to Jud but he would cuss me and abuse me, he would pick some chance to cuss me and abuse me and I didn't say anything to Jud."

"But did he hurt you in any way?" the attorney pressed him.

Wash related an event Daisy told him and nervously said, "Well, Daisy said Jud had made improper proposals to her and told her that she had to make love to him, and she told Jud me and her was going to marry, and Jud said hell no that's my woman, and you leave this damn Wash Smith along if you don't I'm going to kill him."

"Did you speak with Mr. Wells about this matter?" Mr. Cooley said.

Wash tried to stay calm and not show how nervous he was getting and said, "Well, I didn't say anything to Jud about it for it might have caused trouble, for he might have had me worked on the chain gang for working this distillery. I thought I might get caught, he might have me caught and get me in trouble by him having plenty of money and he might have me caught and worked on the road and I didn't say anything to Jud."

Mr. Cooley blurted out, "That is not a reason to take such drastic actions! No more questions."

Wash's attorney looked at the attorney general. He stood to question Wash, "Start from the beginning and tell the court what happened that day?"

Wash began, "All the day this happened I had a Chitwood boy's gun hunting and me and Brock and Freeman happened up over at one of these distilleries that me and the Freeman boy was running that day, well we all commenced drinking and we got pretty full over at this distillery. Well, then we got ready to go home. Freeman said let's go by the store. I want to get some smoking tobacco and I said alright I want something to eat, some can goods."

Wash stopped and his attorney said, "And?"

"Well, we went on up there, and I don't know whether I called Jud or Freeman called him, I wouldn't be positive, but I think Freeman called him up at his house, and he came out, and I remember telling Jud to bring a bowl and some spoons to fix up some can goods," Wash said as he was trying to get all the facts straight in his mind before he continued.

Mr. Barrett asked Wash, "Did he get what you asked for and leave the house?"

Wash nodded and said, "And he come out and brought the bowl, and we went in the store, and as we went in the store; I left the gun at the door, and Brock and Freeman was on the inside of the store setting on the inside arguing about who stole a gallon of liquor from the distillery, and I went on in, and Jud fixed up the can good and sold me a box of shells, and I give him a five-dollar bill, and he gives me back the change in small change."

"And what happened after that?" he said.

Wash said, "And Jud said, 'Wash you got to stay away from Daisy,' and I said Jud did you mean what you said when you said I had to stay away from Daisy, and that Daisy was going to be your woman, and if she wasn't, you would kill me, and he said 'hell yes,' and I started out the door and had picked up my gun and was going home, and Jud said, 'yes, hell I do mean it I'll do it right now!,' and he stooped under the counter, and I thought he was getting his gun to kill me, I knowed he kept his gun under the counter, and that was the words he said, and I shot him and he didn't raise up, and I thought he was still after his gun to kill me, and I shot him again."

The defense attorney said, "You shot him in fear of him taking your life and you defended yourself. So, where did you go afterward?"

Nervously he continued, "And I turned away and went to Chitwood's house and played the Graphophone about an hour and I was getting pretty drunk and I don't remember much after that. And going on over there they shot me and I dropped my gun and it went off and I went on over to Brown's and sometime about three o'clock in the morning Mr. Whelchel and Mr. Wilbanks come and got me and Dr. Holly out here. I think it was Dr. Holly, dressed my arm where it was broke and dressed my other arm where it was shot."

Mr. Barrett asked Wash, "Is there anything you would like to add in your defense?"

Wash said, "Gentlemen, I am a poor boy nineteen years old and had a hard time all my life and had to work from place to place to try and help my mother and I ain't got much education. Jud taught me how to make whiskey and threatened my life and then drawed his gun to kill me and I shot him to save myself."

Mr. Barrett thanked Wash and said he could step down from the witness stand. He was glad the lawyer allowed him to make his last plea to the court before he had to leave. None of the State's witnesses would say anything in Wash's defense. He stood at the witness chair and slowly walked back to the table he had spent most of the last few days waiting. Now, he had to wait for the court to decide the next thing to do.

The judge asked if there were any more witnesses for them to come now. Mr. Barrett did not have another witness and told the judge that he rested his case.

The judge said, "If there are no more witnesses, it is the court's duty to recess so that the attorneys can prepare their closing comment, and I will prepare my statement for the charge of the court to the jury. This court is dismissed."

It relieved Wash that there were no more witnesses and thought that this would soon be over. He knew it had been a strain on his mother. Wash stood, and the sheriff handcuffed him before leaving for the jail. He and the sheriff left the courtroom on their stroll back to the jail. The sheriff could tell that he was very nervous and tried to talk about anything other than the trial. Wash sensed that was what he was doing, but offered very little to the conversation.

As with all the other days, Wash changed back into those baggy prison rags. He thought he had better get used to them and that he would wear them for a while. He did not think these clothes would be what he would wear forever.

He entered his cell and tried to make sense of the situation as he lay on the cot. He would think back to times when they all were together and try to piece something out of all this nonsense. He wondered if pressure from their families had guided the way they acted. Whose family would do such a treacherous thing? He tried to put himself in each one's place, and the only influence so strong towards him was when he felt so intimidated around Jud. He feared what Jud would do to him. He could only account that there had to be some urgency so strong that could affect the lives of so many as much as it had in his own life. He wondered if it was possible if one person or one family could persuade so many.

Could that person or family intimidate all his friends and convince them all toward their way of thinking? What did they fear might happen to them? These questions kept him up much longer than they should. He concluded that fear can override reason. He could not change things and must trust that reason will help. He finally fell asleep and tossed and turned for the biggest part of the night. He woke the next morning as tired as he was when he went to bed. Wringing in sweat the next morning from a restless night, he got out of bed to face the day.

The sheriff returned to give him the suit he had been wearing to the trial. He dressed and ate very little of the breakfast that was brought to him. He told the sheriff he was not hungry and was ready to go whenever he wanted to go. The sheriff told him to stand so he could put the handcuffs on him. Moreover, as he did, Wash thought the sheriff was getting gentler each time he restrained his arms. Walking across the road, the sheriff asked Wash if he was ready to face the day. Wash hoped this trip would be the last time he would have to make it. Lost in his thoughts, Wash crossed the road without thinking. The only thing he wanted to face was his family again. When the two of them entered the courtroom, his mother was already waiting. Wash looked toward her, and she forced a smile to let him know she was fine. Wash was ready to start the fourth day of trial, and he hoped it would be the last.

CHAPTER 14:
CLOSING REMARKS AND VERDICT

The bailiff called the court back to order, and the jury went to their seats. The judge told the lawyer for the State to present his closing remarks. Mr. Cooley stood and walked to the rail in front of the jury. He began, "Gentlemen of the jury, it has been my pleasure to represent the people of Banks County and Georgia. The defendant, in this case, Wash Smith, shot in cold blood Jud L. Wells. It has been this court's duty to present the fact of the case to be simply felonious murder. The defense may argue that the defendant acted in self-defense. The state called, and the witnesses testified and no one presented a case for self-defense. It was the defendant who approached the victim and began attacking him. The defendant attacked him without provocation while he was in his store, filling a request of Mr. Smith. One witness testified that he fled the scene when the posse was there to apprehend him for the crime. He escaped from the officers there to arrest him. Witnesses that were close to him testified there was no prior justification for him to commit such a crime. It was an unprovoked attack on the deceased. At the conclusion of the case, we would ask you to find the defendant guilty that the defense has not met its burden of proof. Thank you."

Wash was glad that his lawyer would stand last to address the jury. He felt that his going last would let each member know he reacted in self-defense. Mr. Barrett stood and adjusted his tie. He walked slowly toward the jury members and did not speak until he was at the rail. He began, "Gentlemen of the jury, this case is about a person who acted out of self-defense. He has testified that the treatment he received from the victim over the last three months was in fear of retaliation that he should not see a specific person. The evidence in this case that the State has presented does not show the true and specific details of the case. It only shows that a person was shot for no apparent reason. But, this is not true. The defendant himself said there had been an issue. Wash Smith acted in self-defense out of fear that his own life was in jeopardy and would be taken from him at that moment. When the victim reached under the counter, Mr. Smith reacted as anyone in this courtroom would when his life is in danger. He protected himself. In collusion of the case, we ask the jury to find the defendant not guilty of murder."

Mr. Barrett thanked the jury for their attention and returned to his seat. Wash could not tell from the expressions on the faces of the jurors how they would decide. He tried to keep up his hopes that the jury would rule in his favor. Unfamiliar with the procedures of the court, he waited blindly in his chair. Wash tried to not let his mind wander and direly tried to hang onto every word the judge was saying.

The judge addressed the jury and instructed them on their duties as members of the trial. He said, "Gentlemen, of the jury, the grand jury of this county returned an indictment against Wash Smith charging him with the offense of murder. It charges that on January 3rd, 1928, Wash Smith committed the offense by murdering Jud Wells, and to that indictment, he entered his plea of not guilty. That is the issue you are sworn and impaneled to do and come to a verdict according to the evidence in the case."

"The defendant enters the trial with the presumption of innocence. The State removes that presumption with testimony sufficient to convince your minds beyond a reasonable doubt of the guilt of the accused. If you cannot, you should acquit after considering all the facts in the case, but if there is no doubt then you should convict. Wash's heart raced uncontrollably in his chest when he heard the judge instruct the jury to convict. The judge's next statement eased his mind somewhat when he said that the true question in criminal cases is whether the testimony is enough to satisfy the mind and conscience of the jury beyond a reasonable doubt of the guilt of the accused."

Wash keeps letting the words of the judge register in his mind when he could calm himself down enough to listen. Wash could not see how any of the jury members could not see that he was in total fear for his life. He heard again the judge say that you are the exclusive judges of the credibility of the witnesses and all the facts and circumstances of the case. The court allowed the defendant to make a statement to the court and jury on his own behalf as he sees fit and proper. This statement is not under oath, and he is not subject to the cross-examined unless he consents. You are authorized to give it just such weight and credit only that you think it is entitled to. You may believe it, or you may reject it.

Wash thought they had to believe it. His friends disappointed him for not backing his testimony more than they did, but his lawyer keeps telling him not to worry. Wash wants to come back to him and say, how can I not worry. His mind wanders back over the last few days and months, and he is lost in his thoughts.

Wash heard the judge tell the jury to consider all the evidence in the case. The judge said, "If you find there is a conflict in the testimony or the evidence and the defendant's statement, it is your duty to resolve that conflict without imputing perjury to any witness. If you cannot, it becomes your duty to believe that witness or those witnesses you think best entitled to believe.

Wash felt that the judge knew the witnesses were not completely honest in their testimony. Why would he be telling the jury that it was their responsibility to resolve the conflict in the stories so that it would not show they have lied on the stand? Wash had worked with most of the witnesses in and around the stills and all of a sudden, not a single person had any recollection of drinking or distilling.

The judge continued and said, "Now, gentlemen, the court will address the law applicable to flight." Wash did not understand why the court was trying to add charges of escape to his case. The judge tried to tell the jury that flight may be an assumption that he was guilty, but that was for the jury to draw a conclusion of guilt or not. Wash thought, why would the judge think that running was due to a sense of guilt? It seemed to him to be the only sensible thing to do at the time. He had not been arrested for anything, so how could he be charged with flight. There were so many things during the last few days that did not make sense to him, and he thought he had one more thing to worry about.

Wash had discovered that whenever the judge started a sentence with, "Now, gentlemen," he was getting the attention of the jury. The judge said, "The defendant is charged with the offense of murder. He goes into a long conversation with the jury, explaining the meaning of murder. Wash knew that murder was the killing of a human being, but he did not think that protecting himself from the same fate was an offense of murder. He so wanted the judge and jury to understand that he did not intentionally take a person's life. Wash thought that under the circumstances, his actions were justifiable. All the time the judge was addressing the jury; Wash thought the judge was trying to convince the jury that he did the shooting with malice, intentional, and without purpose. Wash wanted to protest what the judge was saying, but it was as though his voice had been silenced."

Wash listened to the judge explain to the jury to apply the law of murder if he killed Jud Wells in the manner charged by the intentional use of a gun. Wash sat helplessly as the judge continued, saying that if there were no circumstances of the killing that would excite the fears of a reasonable man to commit such an act, then the act was without justification and he should be found guilty of murder. Wash's thoughts raced back to the store that cold day in January and replayed every incident in that small store. He could not be that wrong in his mind for it to be anything but self-defense. Wash put his hand on his chest and could feel the pounding through his ribs, shirt, and coat. He felt like he had to force air in and out to keep on living. Those shocking words seemed to make his heart stop, but just for a second.

The judge said, "If you have a reasonable doubt as to his quilt, you must give him the benefit of the doubt and acquit him."

The sound of that word 'acquit' made Wash realize that the judge was giving the jury all possible verdicts in the case. Wash listened carefully as the judge continued with his instructions to the jury.

The judge said, "Now, gentlemen, justifiable homicide is the killing of a human being in self-defense, or in defense of one who intends to violently commit a felony upon such person."

Wash heard the judge say that just to be afraid something is going to happen is not sufficient to justify the killing but it must be a total fear that Jud was going to kill him under the influence of those fears, and not in a spirit of revenge.

The judge explains, "The term felony means an offense for which the offender would be subject either to the death penalty or to imprisonment in the penitentiary. Now on the subject of justifiable homicide, if you believe that this defendant did kill, Jud Wells, but if you believe that at that time the deceased was committing a felonious assault or believe that the circumstances surrounding the killing were to excite the fears that the deceased was about to commit a felonious assault upon the person of, Wash Smith and that acting under the influence of those fears, and not revenge this defendant, Wash Smith, shot and killed, Jud Wells, the killing would be justifiable, and you could not convict the defendant of any offense at all."

Wash had a hard time trying to keep up with all the terms and wording the judge was telling the jury. All he wanted for them to understand was that he feared losing his life. Wash was trying to keep his mind on the words at present but it kept going back to the cold store in January.

The judge told the jury that the victim did not have to commit the assault, but Wash acted out of fear and not revenge. The defendant did not intend at all to commit the felonious assault on the victim. The judge said that the killing would be justifiable. The judge included that if you find from the facts and circumstances and conclude at the time of the killing that the defendant believes that the deceased had a weapon and was fixing to kill him and was acting under those fears. Wash wanted to tell the court exactly how it was, but his lawyer told him that was not a good idea at that time.

Wash was deep in thought and was not able to concentrate on what the judge was saying. All he could hear was a mumbling of nonsense words. He would look over at the jury to try to understand what they would recommend, and at his family, he knew what they wanted. His mother wanted it to end and be over, but Wash had committed a crime that was out of her hands and his.

Wash listened and heard the judge say, "After taking into consideration all the facts in the case, together with the defendant's statement, if you are satisfied that the defendant is guilty of the offense of murder, as charged in the bill of indictment, the form of your verdict would be, 'We, the jury, find the defendant guilty.' That would mean the extreme penalty of the law, which is death, would be administered to the defendant."

That last statement the judge said made Wash tremble with a cold feeling all over. He was shaking involuntarily from the top of his head all the way down to his feet. The harder he tried to stop the shaking, the more he quivered, twitched, and palpitated.

The judge continued addressing the jury and said, "The law says the jury trying the case where the defendant is charged with murder can recommend the defendant to the mercy of the court. The punishment would be confinement in the penitentiary for life. And if you should believe the defendant guilty beyond a reasonable doubt, then recommend him to the mercy of the court. The form of your verdict would be, 'We, the jury, find the defendant guilty and recommend him to the mercy of the court."

That statement Wash heard and could feel the tremors easing. He hoped his reaction was not noticed, but when the judge said to recommend mercy, Wash calmed down. The judge continued.

The judge added, "If you are not satisfied of his guilt beyond a reasonable doubt, the form of your verdict would be, 'We, the jury, find the defendant not guilty.' Gentlemen, you may take the indictment and retire to your room and make up your verdict."

It was close to noon and Wash was afraid the judge would recess so everybody could get something for dinner and reconvene to look over the evidence and make the decision that Wash had been looking to get. The jury stood and left the courtroom to the room beside the judge. Wash tried to listen to what the judge was saying, but many times the thought of his words was overwhelming to him. The sheriff looked over at Wash and could tell he was struggling with everything Judge Stark said. Wash had wondered many times how it could be the maximum sentence. He did not want to even think about it. To receive life in prison would be a verdict hard to bear. The sheriff was only doing his duty of watching over Wash for his and others' safety. He was only carrying out his duty as a law officer and not looking at him as a hardened criminal.

As the jury left for deliberation, the judge told the court to recess until the jury returned with its decision. The sheriff had brought lunch in a brown bag for them given to him when Wash's breakfast arrived, but Wash was too anxious to eat and just sat quietly until it was time for the jury to return to the courtroom. His mother did not leave the courtroom but stood gazing out the window, looking across town. Her mind wandered from the last day's events to back over the last several years. Her emotions changed as quickly as her mind did remembering stories through the years. She seemed relieved that Wash did not leave.

He just sat and waited for the decision of his life to be made by twelve men who had listened to every word given by the witnesses. He was sure that there would be a lot of debate before they could make any one decision. The jury deliberated for only a short time and informed the bailiff that they had decided. Wash cannot believe how quickly the jury could reach a verdict. He was not sure if that meant guilty or not guilty. His first thought was that the short time was not a good sign for him. He sat in his chair, trying to keep everything together. His lawyer said there were options if a verdict differed from what they had hoped.

The judge asked that the jury return after deliberation. He instructed the foreman of the panel to rise and asked if the jury had come to a verdict.

The foreman said, "Yes, your Honor, the jury has reached a verdict."

Judge Stark requested the foreman to give him the verdict that the jury decided. He looked at the verdict and handed it to the clerk of court, Mr. Theodore Cheek, and requested, "Mr. Cheek, will you please read what the verdict you have given is based on the facts and testimony of the trial?" The judge instructed Wash to stand as the clerk read the verdict. Wash held on to the table as he waited.

The clerk of the court stated, "The members of this jury find the defendant Wash Smith guilty of murder." Wash had a sinking feeling inside. His mother had been there the entire time and collapsed into her father's arms when the foreman read the decision of the twelve. Wash was visibly distraught over the verdict, but the reaction in the courtroom when those in attendance burst into a loud, uncontrollable reaction made the judge pound his gavel on the desk to get the order back in the court. The judge knew many people in the room were overly pleased with the verdict, but their reaction was not in a manner appropriate for a courtroom. The judge warned the crowd that he would have the courtroom cleared if there was another disrespectful display of emotions.

The judge thanked the jury for their time and dismissed them from the court. The lawyers assured Wash and his family that a retrial would be requested. It was time for them to begin work on that trial. There was a short recess while the judge entered his chamber to prepare his sentencing. Wash was ready to leave but had to endure the eternal wait for the judge to reenter. The words that the jury said devastated Wash. The word "Guilty" kept echoing in his mind. It would not stop. The sheriff put his hand on his shoulder and told Wash to sit in the chair. He wanted to turn around, but he could not look at his mother.

The judge entered the courtroom and was ready to present the sentence to the court. He read, "Whereupon, It is considered, ordered and adjudged by the court, that the Defendant, Wash Smith be taken from this court to the common jail of this county and safely kept there until the day when the sheriff of the county and a guard shall convey Wash Smith to the State penitentiary at Milledgeville, Georgia on April 27th, 1928. The Sheriff of this county shall deliver Wash Smith to the Warden of the State penitentiary where Wash Smith shall be kept safely until the time of the execution of this sentence; and it ordered by the court that, on the 27th day of April 1928, between the hours of 10 A.M. and 4 P.M. the Warden of the State Penitentiary shall inflict the penalty of death by electrocution on Wash Smith within the walls of that State Penitentiary, as by law provided. It is further ordered that said execution be in private and witnessed only by the Warden of the said Penitentiary (who shall be executioner), two assistants, two physicians, an electrician, a suitable guard, and such relatives, friends, counsel, and clergymen as the said condemned person desires......" W. W. Stark signed and filed this statement on March 22, 1928. The judge stood and said, "This court is adjourned."

The entire trial proceeded so rapidly. Sheriff Whelchel handcuffed Wash and led him out of the courtroom and back to his cell across the road. The sheriff did not try to get Wash to talk when they crossed the road. He could tell by the look on Wash's face that it disappointed him with the outcome of the trial. His immense fear covered his face like the mask on an executioner.

The sheriff became more sensitive to Wash's feelings as the time in court progressed. When they got back to the jail, Wash changed back to the prison uniform and thought about what had just happened. He sat in a wooden chair alone in his jail cell for hours, trying to make sense of the chaos. He could not understand how a sentence of such magnitude could come to a person so terrified for his life and was only trying to protect him from being shot. As his lawyer said, "We will file a motion for a retrial immediately." The judge ordered the sentence to be carried out in just two months. He told himself that there has to be enough time to submit the needed paperwork.

Wash was restless that evening. He had a lot on his mind concerning what had happened. Wash thought his life would have gone down a different road. His father had never been an enormous influence in his life. It had always been his mother or his grandfather. Wash thought he would have gotten married and be the head of his household, unlike his father had been. He would be the provider and the protector. It would have been his desire that he and Daisy wed. When he learned that she had married someone else, he thought, how could two people on the verge of getting married to each other get married to someone else so quickly? He decided worrying about that could not control his life and resolved to the fact that she had no other choice. He had his own life to worry about. He feared for his life, and he reacted in self-defense. Now he is fighting for his own life. He keeps thinking that he does not have anyone to turn to for support and protection.

An Atlanta paper published an article giving the details of the trial on March 22nd. Very few people in the county got the paper from Atlanta, so Wash did not see how the paper portrayed him or the trial.

He ate very little of the evening meal that was brought that night. When the sheriff returned to take what he had not finished, Wash asked if he could keep some for later. The sheriff knew he was struggling, so he did not see any reason he could not let him. They talked for a little while, and Wash was glad he did. He stayed up for some time that night and sat in the dark thinking about the last several days. It was late when sleep took over. Wash woke up so many times that night that he could not remember how many. The next morning, he woke up from a dream that terrified him. Even though he was not happy with the place he was, it comforted him to know that the dream was not true.

It was not long before his usual breakfast arrived, and he finally ate most of the food given to him. The sheriff told Wash his lawyer would come by later to go over the paperwork to submit for the retrial. Wash was more at ease hearing the good news the sheriff had just given him. Mr. Barrett came by about 10 a.m. Wash knew things had to be filed within thirty days and to him, that was valuable time he had. When the lawyer finally arrived, Wash was ready to begin the retrial, and the lawyer had started most of the work already. All the lawyer had to do when he got there was to tell Wash what he had drawn up to be submitted. A sigh of relief fell over him when he realized things had already begun.

CHAPTER 15:
REQUESTING A RETRIAL

Mr. Barrett told Wash there were three areas from the trial that were reasons for a retrial. He told Wash that the trial was in error in failing to charge voluntary manslaughter. He said that the charge of flight was irrelevant and immaterial and there was no evidence. The last was that the court failed to consider there to be a previous threat by Jud Wells. The lawyer filed the request for a retrial on March 22, 1928.

Wash waited patiently for the courts and his lawyer to get everything for a retrial worked out. He sat in the cell day after day, wondering how things went. He always felt there to be hope, and one day this nightmare would be behind him. With the lawyer filing the paperwork for a retrial, it delayed the trial. More importantly, to Wash, it also delayed the date of April 27th, his scheduled date to be executed. The courts or the judge denied his first request for a retrial. This news devastated Wash.

Wash found out that the lawyer, Mr. Barrett, had been ill and unable to get out to work on his case. Several hearings had to be postponed until he could resume some of his duties as his lawyer. Mr. Barrett had to send documentation to the court in Banks County, making the judge aware of his illness. He could not get to his office and prepare for his case and had to rely on Early Stark to pick up most of the work and go out and investigate many of the issues and problems during that first trial. The two lawyers got the files submitted in time that the law required.

It was looking like spring, and some leaves were showing on the trees around the courthouse. The sheriff came up to his cell one morning to tell Wash that papers came in to transfer him to the Clark County jail in Athens. He was not sure if the move was one he would like since it would be over an hour for his family to visit. He did not see them as much as he liked, and the move ensured fewer visits. When he got to the Clark County jail, they put him in a cell with other prisoners. Before Clark County jail, he had been in an individual cell. Wash was not sure how he could cope with this change, but like the move, he had no choice.

The Athens Businessmen's Evangelical Club came to the jail just after Wash arrived. The men had been coming to the jail to witness to the prisoners about their salvation. They stopped by and witnessed to each prisoner in the jail. Wash had only spoken to them as they came by for only a few minutes.

The group brought reading material to him, and he always took it and thanked them for coming to visit. They never failed to ask Wash if he had decided about his faith. He told them during one visit that he had done too many bad things to go to Heaven. The men prayed with Wash and told him to read the material. They assured him that no one was too bad that he could not decide. The material gave him a lot to think about, and he was glad they came by his cell.

Wash read the material the Athens Businessmen gave him during the afternoon and evening. He had gone to church when he was small. His mother made sure of that. They attended Mountain View Baptist Church. His mother always called it her home church. Since he had gotten older and was not living at home, he did not go as often as she thought he should.

While he was reading his material, he heard a lot of noise at one end of the jail. He got up to see where the noise was; it turned out to be just a couple of prisoners, arguing and shoving each other. Wash tried to stay out of the way of most prisoners, especially those that were troublemakers. He had enough problems, as he was on his own without the help of others.

Wash sat alone in his cell, and the comments the men from The Athens Businessmen's Evangelical Club had made to him kept coming to his mind. When he told them he had done too many bad things, Wash wondered if he had not gone too far. He told them had made liquor, sold it, and killed a man. Wash could not possibly see how he could make it to Heaven with all he had done.

Wash fell asleep reading the material given to him. He woke up in the middle of a dream that made him feel everything was not lost. He had hope. Wash joined in more of the activities when the Athens Businessmen Club visited. The group came often over the next several months, and Wash had gotten to where he looked forward to their visits.

It would not be until December that the Superior Court would grant a new trial because the judge did not instruct the jury to consider evidence that Wells had made threats against Wash, and that the judge failed to instruct the jury about a possible manslaughter verdict. The court scheduled his new trial for the March term of the Superior Court in 1929. Wash left the details up to his lawyer, hoping he would defend him as far as necessary.

The December news was some of the best news he had received in 1928. He remembered things from a year ago and thought it seemed like only yesterday, but it had been a lifetime away. He remembered planning to get married to Daisy, and her telling Billie Joe about their plans. The good feelings left as quickly as the feelings came when he thought about what Jud had said. He said, "Or else!" That was when his life turned a different path.

Wash got a visit from his lawyer to go over what has been going on for the last little while. Wash sat in his cell most of the time with very little to do to keep busy and to get his mind off the turmoil. His lawyer was a welcome sight to help him catch up on what was going on in Banks County and with his trial. Mr. Stark told Wash that Mr. Barrett could not continue on his case because of medical issues and difficulties of getting out to prepare for the case coming up. So, Mr. Stark said he would try the case in March.

During the first case, Mr. Barrett handled all the questioning during the trial because Mr. Stark had a hearing problem and the two lawyers decided it best that Barrett take care of the questioning of the witnesses. He assured Wash there would be no problems during his upcoming trial. Mr. Stark did not tell Wash, but if he had trouble hearing something during the trial, he hoped he could rely on Mr. Barrett to repeat what he may have not heard. Wash trusted Stark and thought everything was going to be fine.

Early Stark was older than Wash and both enjoyed hunting. When he came to the jail to see Wash, not only did they talk about the case but also about hunting and hunting dogs. Mr. Stark had Setters and Pointers that he bred and raised, and he was always ready to talk about his dogs any time somebody would listen. Sometimes he thought Wash just talked about the dogs to keep him from leaving, but he enjoyed Wash's interest in the animal, and they would talk for a while.

CHAPTER 16:
RETRIAL IN MARCH
1929(PART 3)

When the March term of the Superior Court of Banks County was to start, they transferred Wash from the Clark County Jail back to Banks County. The sheriff arrived just after noon to take him back home, even if only for a day or two he was happy to go. That night, he rested better than he expected. Wash wanted to be at the trial when the jurors were selected so the guard woke him up early to change clothes and get ready for this ordeal.

The sheriff walked with Wash across the road to the courthouse and to Wash nothing seemed to have changed. He saw his family standing to one side of the yard, and he could tell they were upset about something. He wanted to talk to them but the sheriff pointed the way toward the stairs leading to the top floor of the building.

Just like a year ago, the atmosphere around the courthouse was as though there was a carnival in town. People stood around talking about the pending trial. A group of men stood off to one side and seemed to be in a heated discussion about something. Another group across the yard laughed and seemed to be having a good time. One of them seemed to be excited with some of their answers. Wash could not hear what their conversation was about nor see who they were. The only thing Wash could hear was when one of them yelled, "I don't give a damn!"

The sheriff ushered Wash into the room, and they proceeded to the familiar table he sat just about a year ago. His family entered shortly after Wash and occupied the same chairs as before. The only thing between him and his mom was that rail dividing the room.

On March 20, 1929, the court started just like the other one, with Judge Stark officiating. Everything seemed to be the same as last year. The only variation was different jurors and Wash was older. When the bailiff called the court to order, the lawyers started selecting the jurors for this trial. Things progressed as they had the year before. L. J. Bennett was the only member on the jury panel Wash thought he recognized even though he really did not know much about him. Bennett seemed to be pleased that he was placed on the jury. The court appointed him foreman of the jury. Wash wondered if that would be a good sign for him to get a fair chance for a lesser charge.

Wash was anxious but optimistic. He would not let his hopes get too high because of what he had learned when he was there a year ago. Mr. Bennett did not seem to recognize Wash and would not even glance in his direction.

The judge read the indictment of The State versus Wash Smith for murder. "It is in the name and on behalf of the citizens of Georgia, charge and accuses Wash Smith of the county and State aforesaid with the offense of Murder for that the said Wash Smith on 3rd.day of January, in the year of our Lord Nineteen Hundred and Twenty-Eight in the county and State." If the judge said anything after that, Wash was not listening. He had heard those devastating words before, and hearing them again brought back that feeling of desperation and hopelessness.

The judge addressed the jury, "Number 472, The State of Georgia vs Wash Smith; Banks Superior Court, Regular March 1929 term, Trial March 20th, 1929 for murder. The verdict of the trial in the March term of the Superior Court of 1928 was contrary to what the defendant so desired. The results of the verdict were contrary to evidence and without evidence to support it. A new trial was allowed because the court failed to charge the law of voluntary manslaughter, section 65, Penal Code, and because the evidence of P. C. Wilbanks was illegally admitted by the court to the Jury over the objection of the movant showing a charge of flight with no evidence to support. A new trial was also indicated because at the noon hour of the first day of the said trial one juror, T. J. Shubert, strayed from the rest of the jury without the Sheriff. The juror had been impaneled and sworn and evidence in the said case had been taken. He was absent approximately fifteen minutes without the Sheriff during which time said Juror was mixing and mingling with the public at large, there being hundreds of people on the ground around and with him. Wherefore, the defendant prays that these and additional grounds of motion be considered during and throughout the trial."

Wash hoped this trial would go smoothly, and he could get back to some sort of a normal existence in his life. The judge requested the lawyers to present their opening statements, and the proceedings would address the errors from the first trial. The jury members listened carefully to the lawyers' arguments about the errors from the first trial and remedies of the case.

Wash's lawyer was Early C. Stark. Mr. Stark helped his first lawyer, Mr. Finnley Barrett, who was not on the case during this trial because of medical issues he had been having. Mr. Pemberton Cooley again represented the State as the prosecuting attorney. Mr. Stark argued the judge allowed testimony about flight when there was no proof or evidence to that charge during the first trial. He argued the Sheriff had not apprehended Wash at the time he was speaking. He stated that if the sheriff had not placed a person under the control of law enforcement, the State cannot place a charge of flight to the charges. Wash's lawyer also spoke of the use of reasonable force to protect oneself from bodily harm from the attack of an aggressor, if the defender has reason to believe Wash was in danger. He argued that the court did not consider self-defense as an explanation for the shooting and that a retrial was necessary. Finally, the argument about one juror having contact with outside influence after being sworn in as a juror was the fourth issue from the first trial Wash's lawyer brought up.

The judge questioned both lawyers if there was any more discussion and arguments of proof for the charge relating to flight. Both lawyers showed they were both ready to move to the next issue brought before the court, which was an argument about the whereabouts of one of the jury by presenting affidavits from them and individuals attending the case in 1928.

The State presented the affidavit from Theodore S. Cheek, Clerk of the Superior Court of Banks County. The affidavit stated, "That on March 21, 1928, same being the date on which the case of the State vs Wash Smith, charged with the murder of Jud Wells was being tried, at the noon hour after the court had dismissed for dinner and had instructed the officer in charge to keep the jury together and carry them to dinner. I was getting his papers together getting ready to go to dinner myself when the jury trying the case left the courtroom, and a few minutes later saw Mr. T. J. Shubert coming out of the room in which is located the men's toilet and library. Mr. Shubert stopped a few minutes and talked to me, and asked me where the jury went. I told him they had gone to dinner, and he went out the door and went down the opposite side from where the jury went out. There was a sizable crowd there attending the trial, and the court grounds had hundreds of people upon it, and it was impossible for any person to have been there and not come in direct contact with lots of people."Theo. S. Cheek signed the affidavit.

The defense lawyer presented several affidavits stating that the officer did not miss the juror until the group had gone some distance from the courthouse. A jury member called the officer's attention to the fact that a juror was missing. He called for another officer to come and stay with the jury while he hunted up and found the missing juror. The court instructed the jury to keep together and not talk to anybody that is not on the jury and not to allow any person not on the jury to speak to any member of the jury, but Mr. Shubert was away from the jury for some time before the bailiff Mr. Bill Hardy found him and brought him back.

On that day, there were many people in and around the courtroom and in the yard. It would have been impossible for anyone to mix and mingle with the crowd for as long as the juror was absent without coming in contact with friends and relatives of the deceased. A person could not help but hear remarks by people about the trial. Both lawyers for the defense argued that neither of them knew of the irregularities of the procedure at the time that it happened. They presented affidavits to the court and read them to be used at the hearing for a new trial as evidence.

The court discussed the matter of the charge of voluntary manslaughter in the case of The State vs Wash Smith. The State presented its case that from the first trial there was no evidence leading to the fact that Jud Wells had made any threat to Wash Smith at any point before the shooting. Mr. Cooley argued there were no witnesses during that first trial who stated that Mr. Wells had at any point made any terroristic threats toward Wash Smith. Wash acted on his own malicious revenge, shooting Mr. Wells on January 3, 1928.

Wash listened as the problems from the first trial were being addressed. He futilely hoped that the information would help show that it was self-defense. He feared for his life. He saw Will Freeman come into the courtroom; hopeful, he would testify more in favor of him than he did last year.

Mr. Cooley questioned Will to give his account of the events of the murder. Will sat on the witness stand next to the judge's bench and repeated everything just about the same way as a year ago about where he lived in Banks County and how long he had known Wash. Will was older than Jud and had been in the area for a while and knew almost everybody in the area. Especially those testifying in the trial. Wash could tell that Will was more at ease testifying this year and seemed more prepared with his answers. As it was, he had a year to think about what to say.

It was the usual back and forth between the lawyer and the witness. Will would answer the questions about seeing Wash on a brush pile around one or one-thirty, helping Jud kill a hog at Mrs. Smith's at sun up, and when and why they went to the store between four and five. Of course, Will varied little from his previous testimony. Every now and then, he would add information he thought relevant that he failed to mention during the 1928 trial.

When Mr. Cooley asked when did you see Wash again, Will added to last year's statement and said, " He came to my house, my wife and Minnie Wells was there when he came, and he stayed there for about a half an hour, and he went from there to the store. I went with him. He said he wanted to go to the store to get some can goods to eat, and he wanted me to eat some with him, but I told him I had had dinner, but I wanted some smoking tobacco."

Wash did not see why Will thought it was necessary to add that his wife and Minnie Wells were at his house, but he did not see that it added anything to his defense. The state attorney questioned Will about the distance from his house to the store and to Jud's house. The lawyer asked if anyone was with Jud, and Will said Oliver Brock was in the house by the fire.

Wash kept listening to what Will was repeating. Somebody had made a drawing of the store, and Will pointed out where everything and everybody were. Wash tried to see how the detailed drawing would help him build a case for self-defense. Either way, it was part of the trial, and he hoped it would show in his favor. One thing he could see was that the room was so small and only one way out, he had to protect himself if he felt threatened.

Will talked about the can of tomatoes and oysters. Since the store was cold inside, the tomatoes had ice in them. Will told the court that Jud offered to take the tomatoes to the house and warm them for him.

Will continued telling the court that Jud asked him if he salted "the old ladies hog down for her." According to Will, the conversation in the store was nothing more than a casual conversation about what had happened that day and that the tomatoes had ice in them. He added that Oliver was sitting on a bag of grain, Will was at the end of the counter, and Wash was standing about four feet behind him. Will said Jud was about three feet from him and all of a sudden, the gun fired. Mr. Cooley asked what happened after the gun fired, and Will said, " After that gun fired, Mr. Wells just throwed up his hands this way and I understood him to say 'Lord have mercy', and he said something else, but he look like he was choking, and I didn't understand him. He had his hands up like this and he had the little old knife in his hand that he had cut the can goods with and he was just going down like this. I didn't hear Mr. Wells say or do anything to Wash to cause him to shoot him, there wasn't anything said between them that I heard."

It seemed to Wash that the reason he didn't hear anything was he was too busy talking to Oliver at that time about something and had his back to everything. There came a sinking feeling all over him at that time. He was beginning to realize nothing was going to change. Wash wanted the rest of the trial to show his point of reasoning.

Will tried to clear up what happened after the gunshot. He testified that Oliver had made it to the porch of the store and he turned around and yelled, "Lord Have mercy, Wash. What do you mean?" Will thought Wash was going to pull the trigger on him so he ran out the door and did not stop running. About fifty yards away, he heard the gun again and kept running for about a hundred fifty yards when he looked back and saw Oliver running towards him. Will testified that Oliver and Will went to his house. Oliver got Will's gun and went back out. Will said he heard one more shot after Oliver left.

While Will was on the stand, the State lawyer asked Will to give details to the court about the condition of the body and its location after the shooting. None of this testimony was presented in the first trial and Wash could see that the state was trying to persuade the court to make him look like a hardened vicious criminal by giving gruesome details about the bloody scene. Will used the drawing again to show where he stood at the time of the shooting and where Wash and Jud stood. Wash could not help but think about all the danger he faced at that time and the need to protect himself.

Mr. Cooley stopped Will and asked him to tell the court what he did when he left the store and had he seen the defendant again that night. Will testified that Wash stopped by his house about eight o'clock that evening and his son Calloway was with him. Will explained that Wash had been at Sue Smith's house. He told the court that she was sick and it upset her with all the commotion when Wash got there and she fainted. Mrs. Smith asked Calloway to get Wash to leave with him and when the two of them got to Will's house, Wash asked Will what was wrong with all the women folks. Will said he told him they were all scared to death of him. Will said someone should be told that Mr. Wells was dead, and Wash told Will he could not go or he would shoot him. Will told the court that he was scared and that is why he did not tell anyone. Will testified that he did not go back to the store until the next morning.

Mr. Cooley told the court he had no more questions at this time, and Mr. Stark stood to question Will. He intended to get the court and jury to see that it was self-defense for Wash. Wash's lawyer began questioning Will as the state's attorney did. He asked about where he lived, how long he knew Mr. Wells and Smith, and when he saw Wash last. Will continued testifying repeating his residence and how long he had known everyone. Mr. Stark asked Will if he had been working at a still. Will did not seem to want to be connected with a still. Wash thought his lawyer had a good reason for this line of questioning.

Will said, "It's not a fact that me and Wash and Oliver Brock was running one still over there and had met up over there at one still, and my boy and a boy named Curtis Brady and Horace Brady was operating another still in another direction. I have made whiskey when I was a young fellow but not along there. It's been a long time ago; it's been longer than two years. My son and I wasn't helping operate a still over there. I wasn't at a still that day with this boy at no time."

Wash could tell by the way Will was answering the questions that he would not help him prove self-defense. I can only hope for the rest of this trial to prove that murder is not the charge. Will repeated the testimony about where Wash was the first time they met, saying he was on a brush pile. The time between one and four or five is always told differently.

Will tried to clear up Mrs. Smith's name. He was saying that some people called Mrs. Smith, Mrs. Brady, but Smith is her right name. It is the same with her children. Horace and Curtis are sometimes called either Brady or Smith. Wash already knew the reason so hearing one name or the other did not confuse him. It really started back when Joseph's father left and his mother married a man whose last name was Brady. The children were young and everybody just assumed their last name was Brady too.

Mr. Stark asked Will again about when the two of them met before going to the store and what the conversation was once they got there. Will repeated again what he had been telling all alone during the trial that everybody was in good humor and sober. Nothing had been mentioned about a missing gallon of whiskey or about them being in an argument.

Wash heard Will say that nobody had been arguing and that made him wonder where he got that idea. Then he testifies as to the truth that made Wash want to react. But felt the time for any outburst would hurt his chances of a different verdict.

Will said, "Wash came to my house and invited me to go to this store to see him kill a man and we went to Mr. Wells's house and got him to come down there to the store and he cut him some can goods and he just picked up his gun and shot him and there wasn't a word said."

Wash could feel the anger boiling up inside as Will was testifying. He could not see how Will could think that he was invited to go down to the store to watch him kill a man. Killing anyone had not even entered Wash's mind when they had planned to go down to the store. Surely, this will be resolved before the end of this trial. Wash could not see why Will wanted to dwell so much on a jug of whiskey when everybody was testifying there were never any connections to a still.

Mr. Stark continued with his questioning of Will about hearing anymore shots and if the two of them saw each other again that evening. Will would pause and seem to grope for the right words to say and would continue testifying.

Will told the court that Wash came back to his house that evening and sat by the fire and told the court that Wash did not try to hurt him. He only had a shotgun under his arm. Then for no reason, Will told the court that he did not know the reason why the shells were cut.

Will said, "It's not a fact that Mr. Wells cut those shells himself and distributed them to us boys to use at the still, he never did give us any shells."

As Will was finishing his testimony, Wash could not help but think back on that day that changed so many people's lives. Will was retelling the story again of the events inside the small country store. He was talking about things that had been told so many times before. Who bought tobacco, or who ate some oysters? Who entered the store first and where everybody was standing? Wash thought that Will was furiously to avoid any connection to a still. He understood the reasoning why he was doing so.

Will was told there would be no more questions at this time and the bailiff called Oliver Brock. When he passed Will, they did not speak. He nervously came to the front of the courtroom and raised his right hand to be sworn in to testify. He slowly sat in the chair and waited for the state's attorney to question him about the murder.

Oliver Brock began answering the questions that Col. P. Cooley asked by giving his name and where he lived. He said that on January 3rd 1928 he had gone to Mr. Wells' house. He testified that he was at home alone and the two of them sat by the fire for about two hours. Oliver said Will and Wash came by and hollered for Jud to bring some spoons and a dish to the store.

Wash anxiously listened to what Oliver was saying. He was like Will, repeating their version of events, even though there were contradicting facts from everyone. He wonders which version the jury will believe. At least they both agreed on how the store looked with it being made of wood and how wide and long it is. They even agreed about the little porch on the front and the store having one door. Oliver continued and related the tomatoes had ice and opened a can of oysters.

The state attorney asked Oliver what the conversation of everybody was, but Oliver could only remember the part about who killed a hog and who salted it down. Both Oliver and Will avoided any talk about a missing gallon of whiskey. Wash figured that was to draw attention away from making moonshine and that the two of them might not have had their total attention to anything else going on around them. Wash paused in his thinking when he heard Mr. Cooley ask Oliver to describe the events around the time of the shooting.

Wash expected Oliver to go into details like Will did about the scene. All Oliver did was point to his throat and tell the court that the load struck Mr. Wells here and he dropped behind the counter. Oliver said he did not understand Jud to say anything. He did say that Wash told him not to run but he did anyway.

Mr. Cooley asked Oliver if anything was going on between Mr. Wells and the defendant, but he said he did not see Mr. Wells do anything to Wash to cause him to shoot him. Oliver told the court that Mr. Wells did not have any instrument or gun or pistol or anything else in his hand when Wash shot him. There were no harsh words between the two. When he fired the second shot, Oliver fled the store and went out to Mr. Freemans.

Cooley asked Oliver where he went after leaving Mr. Freemans. He told the court that he got a gun from Will and left. Oliver said he saw Wash coming back out the road from the house with his gun but was afraid he would shoot him and ran off. Oliver testified Wash was about a hundred yards from him but he did not say anything to him. Later, Oliver said he heard two guns fire and ran back to the house.

Mr. Cooley walked back and forth in front of the judge's desk then turned to Oliver and asked what he did the next day. Oliver said he went down to the road between the house and store and noticed the kitchen window at the dwelling house had been shot out. Miss Wells was in the house by herself.

Mr. Cooley told the judge that he had no more questions for this witness at this time, and Judge Stark motioned for Wash's lawyer to proceed with his line of questions. Col. Early C. Stark cross-examined Oliver Brock and wanted him to clarify the conversation between Mr. Wells and Mr. Smith on the day of this incident.

Oliver basically told the same version as Will. He said there was not anything said that would cause anyone to shoot another person. Like Will, Oliver wanted to stress that all the talk was about canned goods and nothing was said about a gallon jug of whiskey being missing.

Mr. Stark asked if Mr. Wells had a gun that day since he had mentioned that he had one in the last trial. Oliver said that he did own a gun but did not see one that day.

Oliver said, "I didn't testify before that I saw a pistol out there on the table at Mr. Wells's house."

Wash just shook his head as he listened to more of the events Oliver was telling. Then Mr. Stark asked Oliver if he knew a man named Fitzgerald and a girl named Daisy. Oliver said he did not know a man named Fitzgerald and did not know nor see one they called Blue Bird Fitzgerald, but he knew a girl named Daisy Brady who was Sue Brady's daughter. They live on the Wells' place.

The defense attorney asked if Oliver had been helping Will and Jud kill a hog at the Smiths. Oliver said they did not say where they had killed a hog only that they were salting it down. I came by Mr. Wells because he sent word to me that he wanted to buy the hog that I was killing for myself. We talked for about two hours at his house but did not agree on a price for selling it to him. It was about that time when Jud heard Wash calling him from outside to come down to the store. Will said he wanted to get some smoking tobacco.

Wash listened as the lawyers questioned Oliver. He was telling what he did after the shooting. Oliver only said that he was told not to run, but added that no one tried to hurt him. It was hard for Wash to understand why he said it that way. All Wash thought was that he was only trying to defend himself from Jud. Wash was upset that none of the questions led to showing that he was in fear of his life. Wash did not feel there was a need for him to protect himself from Oliver or Will. They both knew they were in no danger of being hurt. It was Jud that posed a threat in his mind. Oliver told the court that he went down to Will's house and got his gun and went back out.

Oliver answered that Mr. Smith did not come down to Will's house when he was there. After they left the store he went to Will's for a gun. He said he did not look to see if it was loaded. He just got it and left. Oliver said when Wash went back down to Will's house he was home. He repeated what he told the state lawyer about his reasoning for going down to check on Miss Wells. This time he went into details about his gun would shoot six times but the one Wash had would only shoot twice. Other than that, his remarks were the same.

Mr. Stark indicated to the judge that he had no more questions for Mr. Brock. The judge asked the plaintiff if there were any more questions for this witness. Oliver stood and left the courtroom.

The judge decided to break and recess until after lunch. The next witnesses to be questioned would be the sheriffs from Habersham and Banks Counties and their testimony would begin when everybody got back from the lunch recess. Wash was ready to flee because the testimonies of the witnesses he once called friends did not help him feel as if anything was going to change. Wash stood and the Sheriff put handcuffs on him and the two of them left for the cell across the road. Wash and Sheriff Whelchel did not talk on their way to the jail. Wash did not want to know what he thought the lawyers would ask the two sheriffs.

When they got back to the jail, the two of them stayed downstairs in the sheriff's office. Sheriff Welchel brought two ham biscuits from home. He gave Wash one for lunch. He thanked the sheriff and slowly ate it. It was not long at the jail when it was time to go back to the trial. Whelchel and Wash left for the trial and as they walked across the road. Wash looked around at the familiar sights of home. He looked at the stores close by and the boarding house across the road. The buildings were still very much a part of the old town. People in and out of the businesses buying things they could not grow or make at home. Purchasing plows, sugar, and mason jars loading the items in a wagon or an old black truck.

The two entered the courtroom and proceeded to the familiar place they occupied during both trials. After everybody that was part of the trial was in place, the judge entered the room. The room was silent and each step the judge took seemed to make the wood in the floor strain and crack. The noise of the floor stopped when the judge took his seat behind the regal looking desk at the front of the room. Wash did not notice that sound before. This time it was so noticeable. It reminded him of the old floors at home, at Sue's and the store. The judge hit the desk with his gavel and called the court to order. The clerk called the first witness for the second day of the trial.

The next witness P. C. Wilbanks was called and duly sworn in to testify. He was directly examined by Col. P. Cooley. Wilbanks was the Sheriff of Habersham County and had testified at the trial last year. He stated that he got a call from the Cornelia Bank about the shooting needing him to come down and help search for the man that killed him. He went to the Cornelia Hardware and got his deputy before going down to Banks County. Wilbanks told the court that he and the posse went into the storehouse and saw the body. The body had slipped down and fell back against the wall and had his knife gripped in his right hand.

Sheriff Wilbanks continued with his testimony giving a detailed account of the condition of the body, where the body was shot and where, as he put it, the parties involved had gone. Much of what he was testifying to was the same from a year ago. He did add a few more details but nothing more that would help the jury be convinced that it was a shooting in self-defense.

Mr. Cooley asked the sheriff when he first saw the defendant. He said it was about two miles from Mr. Wells. The posse had to leave the public road and go across a rough field. At the house they went to, no one was home, so they returned and were about a quarter of a mile from the highway when the posse heard two shots coming from the Wells' place. That was when the posse divided into three groups.

The sheriff continued by telling about where everybody was on that lonely moonlit country road that night when the posse was looking for Wash. When they heard someone coming down the road, he explained how they all scattered around in the ditch against the bank. The posse could hear footsteps and when he got even with the men he stopped and throwed his gun up toward the posse. So much of the testimony was a complete repeat of the first trial.

The sheriff continued with his testimony and said that when they met up with Mr. Smith, he was watching us and said what big long legged son of a bitch is out there. Mr. Hill, a posse member, told him to drop his gun but Hill and Smith fired about the same time. Mr. Smith's gun would not fire and he threw it down and ran. Wash had taken an old ridge road and the posse hunted him for about an hour. They tried to track him through the field, but it was an awful, cold night and ice was spewed up all over the ground. The posse decided to wait until morning and went back to where the man was killed. We were there only a few minutes and someone came running in and said Wash Smith was down at Wiley Brown's. They had sent for a doctor because he was shot up pretty bad. The sheriff said when they took charge of him he was in bed.

Mr. Cooley told the judge he didn't have any more questions at this time and Wash's lawyer stood and asked the sheriff to explain the reasons for cutting a gun shell.

Col. Early C. Stark cross-examined Sheriff Wilbanks and asked him to explain the meaning of a shell being cut. The sheriff explained that the only effect of cutting shells would be to make a close pattern of the shot. If a person shot at a spot, it would cause a more even pattern with it than with a shell that had not been cut. He explained that any kind of twelve-gauge shotgun shells in shooting at a distance of about twelve or fourteen feet the buckshot will stay together. It is for long distance shooting that a cut shell is needed, it will hold together better.

For a while during the trial, the two lawyers were up and down questioning the sheriff from Habersham County. Wash didn't see why his testimony meant so much to either lawyer, but his testimony about the entire search by the posse seemed to be of utmost importance. Wash wanted to get back to the testimony that pertained to him fearing for his life and acting in self-defense. The part of the testimony he earnestly wished he could change.

Finally, the lawyers were satisfied with the sheriff's statements and the judge told him to step down. The judge called for S. J. Whelchel the sheriff from Banks County came to the stand and was duly sworn in.

Col. P. Cooley asked, "Can you please state your name and what you remember on January 3rd, 1928?"

Mr. Whelchel stated," I am Sheriff of Banks County, I remember on about January 3rd, 1928 being called on to go to Mr. Jud Wells Home and I went and my boy Clarence with me. I don't know what time of night or day it was when I was called but it was somewhere around eleven o'clock at night when I got there. I went to Mr. Jud Wells and I saw him in the little store there."

So much of what the two sheriffs were telling did not vary much from the year before. Wash tried to listen to see if anything was not the same as they told earlier and if their recollection was the same. Mr. Whelchel told what happened when the posse got to the house where Wash was. The sheriff said that Mr. Brown was trying to make a fire in the fireplace and Wash was in the back room lying in bed. Wash remembered being told to get up but had a struggle getting out of bed and told the sheriff he could not because he had been shot. The sheriff searched Wash and found gun shells in his pocket. The shells and some money he had in his pocket and the broken gun he had on the road were turned over as evidence as soon as they got back to Homer.

The sheriff mentioned that Jud had a hat on and said that it was blown apart from the shooting. The hat had been missing since the time Wash was taken to the jail and booked. The sheriff said his son took it to the jail and the black woman that cleaned the jail must have taken it out in the trash and burnt it. It could not be found to be brought in as evidence.

Mr. Cooley told the judge he had no more questions for this witness at this time and Col. Early C. Stark cross-examined Sheriff Whelchel. Mr. Stark asked the sheriff to describe the wounds that Mr. Smith had.

Sheriff Whelchel said, "Both bones on this boy were broken along here, he was shot, and he was shot somewhere along here is all, a flesh wound up here, and I believe there was a flesh wound on one of his sides, he had four wounds in his body. Both bones were broken in his right arm and he was wounded in the side. The doctor said his collarbone wasn't broken. Dr. Holly dressed his wounds."

Whelchel continued and told the court that it was around eleven o'clock at night when they got to where Mr. Wells' body was. There were several people in and around the building and none of them seemed to be afraid to go up to the house. The sheriff said while they were outside two men drove up in a car inquiring for Mr. Wells that night.

Sheriff Whelchel told the court and Mr. Stark that two men drove up in a car asking for Mr. Wells. The lawyer wanted to know if it was Mr. Fitzgerald, and the sheriff said he did not know Mr. Fitzgerald. He said he was an unusually tall man. The man asked for Mr. Wells and the sheriff showed him where he was. The sheriff added that he drove an automobile that looked like a high priced car. I couldn't tell much about it because it was dark but the moon was shining and it looked like a high priced car.

When the examination was redirected by Mr. Cooley who wanted to know if Mr. Wells was alive at that time, the sheriff answered him saying that Mr. Wells was dead that time and had been dead for several hours. The lawyer had no more questions, and the sheriff stood and came back to sit next to Wash. Neither one looked at each other but Wash knew he was testifying his part in what had happened.

Judge Stark decided to recess for the day. He instructed the jury on what to do before leaving and told them not to have any contact with anyone not involved with the case. He did not want a repeat of any issues with the jury as he did in the March 1928 trial. Judge Stark told the lawyers and jury members to resume at nine o'clock the next morning.

The sheriff stood to take Wash to the jail across the road. He handcuffed him and they walked slowly out the door and down the stairs facing the road. Wash thought the stairs seemed steep. It was always hard to go up and down the stairs being handcuffed and the sheriff, as always, held Wash by the elbow to help steady him. The sheriff worried that Wash would trip and fall. As steep as the wooden steps were, a person could break an arm or leg rather easily. The sheriff did not think Wash needed another problem at the moment.

When they got in the cell, Wash changed back into his prison clothes and waited for someone to bring supper. He sat on his cot for a long time and thought about the testimony of today. He was convinced that his hope for a lesser sentence did not rest in the hands of the two sheriffs that testified, but in those of his so-called friends. He wrestled with these ideas in his mind and could see how people and his situation had changed in one long year. Nothing he could do at that moment but wait.

The sheriff brought his supper in the late afternoon and told Wash he would check on him before he left for the day. Wash ate some but fell asleep before the sheriff came back. He finally drifted to sleep late in the night, and the sheriff came to wake him early the next morning. He brought him a biscuit and a cup of coffee but since it was not time to leave he did not wake him but placed what he had brought on the shelf in the cell door.

When Wash woke up, a biscuit and coffee were in the opening in the jail door. He had breakfast, dressed before eight, and drank his coffee until the sheriff came to handcuff him and leave in time to get to the courthouse and trek up the steep steps before the judge instructed everyone to be there.

It was a lonely sad walk for him back across the road. He knew Wiley Brown would begin the day and did not feel that his testimony would sway any hopes toward a lesser sentence. Everything was as usual when they got to their place in court. Wash turned his head to the sheriff when he spoke and gave him an excuse to not speak or acknowledge Wiley. The judge called the court to order and the process began.

The judge called Wiley Brown to the stand to be duly sworn in. The State's lawyer asked him to give his name and what he was doing on January 3rd. Wiley did not vary far from his testimony from 1928. Wiley was about the same age as Wash and both had known each other for several years. Wiley lived with his parents on Ruff Moses place, which was about a mile from Jud's house and store. Ruff was Jud's uncle. Wash got to Wiley's house about twelve or one o'clock at night and told them he had been shot up and could Wiley go for the doctor. Wiley testified again that the doctor lived a short distance away to get the doctor to go to his house. Wiley ran into Jud's brother Gus and said Wash sent him out to get the doctor. Gus went over to Jud's and told the two sheriffs where Wash was. They proceeded there to arrest Wash.

The lawyers both said no more questions and Wiley was allowed to stand and leave. Wiley was uncomfortable having to testify in a court of law and Wash listened carefully to what was being said. He, Wiley, and Calloway were all about the same age and had known each other for a while. Calloway Freeman was the next to be called to the stand to be sworn in.

Mr. Cooley and Mr. Stark questioned Calloway. He testified that on January 3, 1928, he had gone earlier in the day with Horace Smith to Baldwin to get medicine for Horace's mother. When the two of them got back home, Wash was at Sue's house. With all the excitement that happened when Wash came over, Sue was not feeling well and fainted from the chaos. Several people lifted her to carry her outside for some air. Sue asked Calloway to get Wash to leave and to tell him to go with him to get her some medicine. Wash got his double-barreled shotgun and left with Calloway. They went about a quarter of a mile to Delmar Chitwood's.

Calloway told the court that Wash ate supper and after eating went to the hearth and counted his money. They stayed about half an hour to an hour before the two left. Calloway said they went to the store and Wash tried to get him in the store to look at the body. They struck a match to see inside and Calloway said he could see the body but Wash went to the shelf and took two boxes of shells from there and was ready to leave.

Calloway's testimony was in a little more detail than in 1928, but he told the same thing he and everybody else had been telling. There were no more questions for Calloway and the court had G. B. Stevens sworn in to testify.

Mr. Stevens was in the furniture and undertaking business in Cornelia. Stevens testified the condition of the body when he arrived and the position it was found. He reported that Mr. Wells had a knife in his hand firmly grasped. He said that Mr. Wells was buried at Level Grove in Habersham County. He said he did not see any weapons around the body except the knife in his hand. Mr. Stevens added in his testimony the size of the wounds and described what kind of shot could have made that kind of wound.

Mr. Stark had two more witnesses to question about a letter that Daisy had written. The court called

Mrs. Ruby Smith and Mrs. Allen Avery to testify. Mrs. Ruby Smith said Daisy had written a letter to her daughter Mrs. Allen Avery and got it on Christmas Eve day of 1927. Mrs. Smith testified that she knew Daisy wrote the letter to her daughter. She said she had shown the letter to Wash and laughed at him about it and said that was why he knew she had gotten a letter. She stated that the letter had gotten lost and could not find it to bring to court.

When Mrs. Allen testified all she could add to the testimony was that she did get a letter from Daisy that was in this envelope and she did not know what happened to it. She was sick at the time and did not try to keep up with the letter. The lawyer told her to step down from the stand.

Mr. Cooley told the judge that the state rests. All the witnesses that had gotten to the court by the state were questioned. It was now time for Wash's lawyer to prove his case of self-defense. Mr. Stark stood and told the judge that he was ready for his first witness. Wash's lawyer had four men subpoenaed to give testimony about the truthfulness of the state's main two witnesses, Freeman and Brock.

The purpose was to let the court know that under oath neither of the two could be trusted to tell the truth or at least that was what the defense lawyer wanted to prove. B. J. Wilkinson was sworn in and testified that he had lived in the county for over fifty-eight years and the general reputation of both men would be considered bad. He testified that Will Freeman was indeed a farmer but could not say what other occupation he had around there. Of course, everybody in the courtroom knew that Mr. Wilkinson was implying that they had worked in the distilling business.

Wash's lawyer called Morgan Evans and then Willie Simmons after Mr. Wilkinson left the stand. The two of them gave just about the same type of report about Freeman and Brock. Morgan Evans said that Will Freeman was a terrible lie teller, and Willie Simmons said that Oliver Brock would swear a lie is true. It was the general agreement that both men at one point in their life did make liquor even though they both swore under oath they never did. The fourth man, 72-year-old Franklin Rice, took the stand and then reported that he only knew Will Freeman and only knew Oliver Brock when he saw him.

Rice said, "I don't know their general reputation."

When both lawyers had questioned the men concerning the character of the main two witnesses, the judge asked if there were any more to take the stand. Neither lawyer had any more questions for Willie Simmons and the judge recessed for an hour to get lunch. Most everybody stayed put in the courtroom and only left for a moment to go to the bathroom or to smoke. The jury went to the room behind the judges' desk for a break and a bite to eat. The afternoon session started promptly an hour after the recess.

When the session started, Judge Stark asked Wash if he would like to add a statement before continuing the trial.

Wash went to the stand and sat in the chair next to the judge. Wash said, "Well, gentlemen, about two months before this thing happened I hired to Mr. Wells by the day. He put me and Will Freeman and Oliver Brock and Dudley Ayers making liquor over there for him and he put Horace Brady and Curtis Brady and Calloway Freeman operating another still. Well, we was running two stills as I told you last court. And Mr. Whelchel sent his deputy up there during last court or just after court and he found the two stills just as I said and the two stills had been moved but the barrels and boxes were there just where I said they were and his deputy knows I told the truth about that."

"So I knowed Mr. Wells all my life but this was the first time I ever made any liquor for him or ever worked for him, but of course, I knowed he had been making liquor several years. Well he had a family living down there on his place by the name of Brady, she went sometimes by the name of Smith and she had several children, and some folks said the children belonged to Mr. Wells. She had a daughter named Daisy that didn't belong to Mr. Wells though, and I had been going with this girl for some time and would have married her if this thing hadn't happened. And Jud had been mad at me for something but I didn't think anything of it. I just went on and didn't say anything to him. Well, Daisy told me that Jud had made improper proposals to her but I didn't say anything to him about it for I knowed he had me making liquor for him and he had me where he wanted me. The day this thing happened, me and Mr. Freeman and Mr. Brock, we met up at the still where Horace Brady and Calloway Freeman, and Curtis Brady was making liquor at the still. e stopped over there a little bit and drink some beer and when we got ready to go Mr. Freeman said let's go by the store I want some smoking tobacco and I said alright I want some can goods to eat and so we went on up there and I won't say who called Mr. Wells out, I won't say which one of us did, but one of us called him and he come out there and we went to the store and as we went in the store I set my gun down on the outside of the door and Jud went in behind the counter and Brock was back over here and Will Freeman was standing back here and I was right here and Brock and Will Freeman was back there arguing about who had taken a gallon of liquor from the still that day. Well me and Mr. Wells was back here and he fixed some can goods for me and I give him a five dollar bill and he give me the change back for it and Mr. Wells said to me Wash you got to stay away from Daisy, and I said Jud did you mean what you said about Daisy going to be your woman and if I didn't stay away from there you was going to kill me and he said hell yes and he struck at moreover the counter and I struck back at him and he stooped down under the counter where I knowed he kept his pistol all the time and he said yes god damn you if you don't believe I will do it I will do it right now, well I had my gun setting back out here and when he made for his gun I stepped up here and reached and got my gun from outside the door and shot as quick as I could and when I shot he was still down under the counter, I thought he was still after his gun and I thought he was going to kill me like he said he was, well I up with my gun and shot this way, the counter was this way in there and the door was right here and Jud was here and I was right here and I just up and shot this way, I thought he was going to kill me like he said. Well, that was just the actual words that was said and the licks that was passed."

"And Mr. Freeman and Mr. Brock knows they got up on this stand and swore false against me, I have sworn the truth all the way through, that is just like it happened and they knowed this liquor business is just like I have told it, they swore false against me either on account of fear of the Wells family or for money."

"And Blue Bird Fitzgerald come up there that night to get a load of liquor and he was up there the week before and got a hundred gallons of liquor and gentlemen that is the way it was. I shot Jud to save my life; I thought he was after his pistol when he reached down under the counter. And gentlemen the only way a poor boy can get a just verdict is to get a jury that won't be bought. I learned Mr. Presley and Mr. Ruff Moses had been to the jury trying to buy them to make a verdict against me and I learned that Mr. Donaldson had been to my lawyer and tried to hire him to quit me but he has been faithful to me all the time. And this thing happened just like to have told you and Freeman and Brock swore false against me either from fear of the Wells family or pay one and I am a poor boy and I hope you will let me go home to my mother."

"Now something has been said about the shells being cut, the shells were cut up there Christmas when I was shooting at a spot and I didn't have any intention of shooting Mr. Wells until this thing happened there in the store, and I did not tell Wiley Brown to go up there and he would find his brains in his hat. He swore false either from fear of the Wells family or for money one. The whole bunch that swore against me has either from fear or for money; they are willing to swear false and send an innocent man to the electric chair to death for money or fear. So gentlemen all I ask of you all is to give me justice in this case, that's all I want is justice."

Wash looked at the judge and indicated that was all he had to say at that time. His lawyer motioned for Wash to return to his chair beside the sheriff and told the court that the defense rests.

After the defense rested, David Nunnally was called to testify and was duly sworn in. Mr. Cooley asked the general questions to a witness. Nunnally told the court that he was deputy sheriff in his district and lived around three miles from Jud Wells. He had gone to Jud's house that night after he was shot and had gone upstairs to his room and found a 38-caliber pistol. He testified that he did not search around the body for any gun and did not see one at the store.

The defense attorney Mr. Stark asked, "Can you explain more about Mr. Wells' pistol?"

Nunnally said, "I don't know who carried that gun from the store up there and put it on the table."

The defense attorney said, "No more questions for this witness."

Wash heard every word that Mr. Nunnally said. He was hopeful that this testimony would help his plea for self-defense. Wash settled down and was able to concentrate more on what the coming witnesses had to say.

The state now brought in witnesses who swore to the honest and truthfulness of Will Freeman and Oliver Brock. It was important for the state to dispute some of the testimony from earlier witnesses who stated that neither could be trusted in anything they would say. The state introduced three witnesses, A. J. Martin, the bailiff from the Columbia District of the county, and two residents of the county, Benton Norton, and J. E. Vinson who all knew Freeman and Brock. It was the consensus of the men that the general character and reputation of Freeman and Brock were above average and none had a reason not to believe either whether they were sworn to oath or not. It was also thought that if they manufactured whiskey they had no knowledge of them working at a still and had no bearing of them not believing the witnesses.

Col. P. Cooley called Delmar Chitwood to the stand and he was duly sworn in to testify. Wash had been living with Delmar for a month or two before Christmas and had been helping him with the crops and chores around the farm. Wash had promised to raise a crop for the coming year as his keep on the farm. Delmar told Mr. Cooley that he was not aware of any business that Wash had with Mr. Wells or any arguments between the two. The State's lawyer asked if he had made whiskey for Jud Wells, and Delmar told him that he was not aware of

Wash manufacturing whiskey or any other work he may have done for Mr. Wells.

On cross-examination by Early C. Stark, his questioning was more concerned about the moonshine and asked, "Did you and Wash manufacture whiskey to sell to a Mr. Kemsey?"

Delmar protested and said, "It's an unfair question to ask me if before he went to work for Jud if I and he had made some whiskey. It's not concerning this case whether Mr. Kemsey from Gainesville got 480 gallons of whiskey from my house on Thanksgiving night."

Delmar wanted to set it straight that he had no part in distilling moonshine. Both lawyers had no more questions for him. At this point, the state wanted Will Freeman to be called back to the stand in an attempt to clarify some of the testimony over the last two days. Since he had already been sworn in, Mr. Cooley motioned for him to have a seat next to the judge's desk and he asked Will, "Were you aware of any gun that Mr. Wells had at the store?"

Will said, "Jud didn't keep any gun or pistol or anything of that kind to shoot with around his store to my knowledge, he kept his firearms upstairs."

That answer seemed to satisfy Mr. Cooley. He told the judge that was all for now and Wash's lawyer Mr. Stark stood and asked Will since he had heard the testimony about the gun Mr. Wells owned was he sure there was no gun in the store other than the gun Mr. Smith had.

Will testified that he was at the store a lot and had never seen any gun that Jud owned at the store. The only gun he had was a long range 32 that one of his nephews gave him. He kept that gun on the table in his room. Will described the gun as a Smith and Wesson with a four-inch long nickel-plated barrel. He told the court that he was in Jud's room a lot of times, and whenever it was raining, Jud's sister would tell Will to go up to his room.

Will stated, "If he had had it in his pocket, I couldn't a seed it. It wasn't under the counter; they got it up in his room that evening. I don't know who all was there that could have taken it up there between four in the evening and eleven o'clock that night. I know he kept one right there by his bed and when I saw it he had a big Smith and Wesson lying there on the table."

Wash was glad Will was called back to the stand. Even though he was unsure if his testimony would help prove self-defense, it did indicate there could have possibly been a gun at the store. Mr. Cooley and Stark both changed the direction of their questioning. Mr. Cooley seemed to be more concerned with questions related to whether or not Wash paid for the tomatoes and oysters and did he get any shells. Mr. Stark was more concerned with Will and Oliver fussing over a missing gallon of whiskey. Will said that he did not care what Oliver swore to that night and then said something about Wash coming by his house with Calloway and sitting around the fire warming. Will said he had not gone for the sheriff but stayed home trying to calm down his kids who were scared.

Col. Stark told the judge he had no more questions for the witness, and Will was told he could step down. Wash felt more at ease than from the first trial and hoped that the jury would see that he was in danger of his life being taken. He had lived in fear for some time thinking that Jud would make good on his statement. He wondered when Billie Joe Brown would be called in as a witness. Then, he would feel like things would be better.

The defense attorney stated they were ready to call Billie Joe Brown to the witness stand. The attorney for

Wash issued a subpoena for her to be present at this term of Superior Court in Banks County. It stated she was a material witness and could verify the charge that Jud Wells made the statement about him threatening the life of Wash Smith if he did not stay away from Daisy Smith. The defense learned that Miss Brown was not available for the court, and the sheriff had failed to serve the subpoena to her before the beginning of court. There had to be something that changed her mind about coming to testify for Wash. He knew that Billie Joe and Daisy had been close friends, and he thought she would help Daisy and Wash prove self-defense. He thinks back to March in 1928 during the first trial, and Daisy did not support his defense at all. Wash thought that Billie Joe changed her mind about coming or did someone pressure her to change her mind. It must be the same with both Daisy and Billie Joe. The thought came to his mind, as he was really on his own.

Wash was counting on Billie Joe to verify his claim that Jud threatened his life if he did not leave Daisy alone. She was his sole witness hoping to prove his case of voluntary manslaughter as self-defense. He did not have a good feeling about how things were developing in his case. He felt like this entire trial was a waste of his time. It has not helped him to prove self-defense. Even if they dropped the charge of flight, not having proof that Jud threatened his life would make no difference in his case; Wash was at a loss. A feeling of desperation came over him. Panic was about to overcome him, and his lawyer told him they could put a motion before the courts to have her appear. Wash put his trust in his lawyer.

The judge called for a recess since it was around three in the afternoon and told that court would resume in thirty minutes when the lawyers would begin with their closing statements. The sheriff told Wash to stand so that they could walk across the road to the jail. The sheriff hardly spoke on the way back to the jail. Wash had a lot going on in his mind about the day and did not answer when the sheriff asked him questions. The sheriff removed the handcuffs from his arm even though they would not be there very long. When it was time to head back to the courtroom Wash put his hands behind his back for the sheriff to put on the handcuffs, and they crossed the road again with little conversation. Wash looked back across the town toward the east and where his home was and wondered if everybody was fine. The thoughts made him homesick, and he wondered if he would ever see the place again. Wash was not one to cry, but tears streamed down his face when he thought about family and home.

Wash and the sheriff went up the stairs to the upstairs courtroom and opened the large white wooden door into the room. The two of them went to the table on the left of the courtroom. He turned his back to the sheriff so he could take off the handcuffs and hoped he would not see the tears. As soon as the sheriff took off the handcuffs, Wash dried his eyes with the cuff of his shirt. He suspected the sheriff knew what he was doing. The sheriff just smiled and nodded to him to sit when Wash finally looked his way. He never let on.

The judge entered, and the bailiff called the court to order, and the judge asked Mr. Cooley for his closing remarks. He stood as before and argued to the jury about his case for a maximum penalty of the law. His remarks were short compared to before, but just as vicious. Wash was glad his lawyer spoke last and hoped that his argument would show the need for a lighter sentence. The judge gave his charge to the court when both lawyers finished their closing statements. His remarks were like what Wash could remember from last year. He repeated the instructions to the jury to charge according to the evidence from the trial. They were to return a verdict of not guilty if the evidence presented was true and insufficient to prove murder and if there is reasonable doubt. If the evidence of the trial proved sufficient and without a reasonable doubt to the guilt of the defendant, the judge instructed the jury to return a verdict of guilty. The jury stood and left the room.

The judge called a recess for the time needed for the jury to reach a verdict. Wash could not or did not want to predict the outcome. He was completely wrong the last time. He just sat in the chair, gazing out the window toward home. Time passed slowly, but he was fine with that. He did not want the jury to come back so quickly as they did at the last trial. When the jury finally entered, the foreman announced to the bailiff that the jury had reached a verdict. Mr. Bennett stood and handed the paper to the clerk of court and the judge read the verdict. Judge Stark handed the verdict to Mr. Cheek and instructed Wash to stand while the clerk read the verdict. Mr. Cheek read, "We, the jury of the Superior Court of Banks County March 1929 term, find the defendant Wash Smith guilty of murder."

The judge read the sentence of the court. Judge Stark states, "Whereupon, it is considered, ordered and adjudged by the court, that the Defendant, Wash Smith be taken from this court to the common jail of this county and safely kept there until the day when the sheriff of the county and a guard shall convey Wash Smith to the State penitentiary at Milledgeville, Georgia, and shall be not before the 30th day of April 1929 and not later than the 1st day of May 1929. The Sheriff of this county shall deliver Wash Smith to the Warden of the State penitentiary where Wash Smith shall be kept safely until the time of the execution of this sentence; and it ordered by the court that, on the 3rd day of May 1929, between the hours of ten A.M. and four P.M. the Warden of the State Penitentiary shall inflict the penalty of death by electrocution on Wash Smith within the walls of that State Penitentiary, as by law provided. It is further ordered that said execution be in private and witnessed only by the Warden of the said Penitentiary (who shall be executioner), two assistants, two physicians, an electrician, a suitable guard, and such relatives, friends, counsel, and clergymen as the said condemned person desires......" W. W. Stark signed and filed this statement on the 22nd, day of March 1929.

The judge stood and said, "I adjourn this court."

Wash sat in the chair. He did not realize that he had slowly lowered himself into it without thinking. His mind was echoing the verdict repeatedly, just as it was a year ago. What am I to do? These were his only thoughts. His lawyer said that he would again request a retrial because of the key witness not showing up for court. Billie Joe Brown was his only eyewitness willing to testify for Wash to the statement Jud made. Someone had to find her and bring her to speak on his behalf. Wash thought about how so many things could go wrong during his defense? Things did not add up, and he prayed his lawyer would discover how so many problems seemed to arise throughout the trial. He just had to clear up this misjudgment.

Wash only saw his mother on the last day of the trial. She could not get there for all of it, but Wash was glad for what time she was there. He just thought that the trial was too much for her to bear again and only came after she heard the trial was in the hands of the jurors. Wash went back to the jail and waited for the time to leave for Athens. The sheriff told Wash they would leave the next morning for Athens and for him to change clothes and rest until it was time to go. Wash was not at all ready to go back to Athens, so what the sheriff said about staying the next day was a relief. Wash was awake most of the night and only slept periodically. The night seemed to draw on forever, and when the sheriff came to wake him; he was already dressed.

Wash spent most of his day, just as he did the day before, sitting and waiting. He often thought back to the farm in Banks County and wondered what was happening. He did not get many visits from his family. Once the trial was over, Wash felt like all his hopes were gone. The sheriff came up and told Wash he had a visitor. He could not think who would be coming. It turned out to be his niece Emma and her son Edward came to Homer and stopped in to check on how he was doing before they left for home. The sheriff let them go up to his cell and talk as long as she could stay. Edward always enjoyed it when Wash came to visit them at home. Wash spent time with the little boy talking about hunting and fishing. When he came up the stairs to see Wash, he ran up to the bars. He was not sure about what he saw when he got in there but quickly forgot and asked questions, as all kids do. Wash dragged his chair close to the bars and put his legs through so he could let Edward sit on his lap. This visit did Wash more good than anything did in the last several months.

Occasionally, he got visits from his lawyer, but a visit from family was always special. He was so sad when they had to leave. Before she left she told Wash about what she heard in the courtyard the morning before the trial. She said some men were talking about the trial and made comments about Wash deserving the charge of murder. She said she did not think much about it at the time but the man that made the remark happened to be appointed as the foreman of the jury.

He hugged them through the bars and pulled his chair back so they could not see how much he was hurting when they had to go.

The deputy came up to tell Wash later in the morning that he would leave about one in the afternoon, so he would have time to do what he wanted before the sheriff and Wash left Homer. Wash's lawyer stopped by his cell before they left and told Wash that he had started the paperwork for a request for a new trial. Wash told him what he had learned from his niece, and he assured Wash he would check out the story and let him know how that may have influenced the trial. The sheriff came back when it was time to leave and unlocked the cell door for Wash to come out. He turned around for the handcuffs, and they left for Clark County Jail. His time at home was not as long as he had hoped, but at least he saw family.

Another article came out in an Atlanta paper on Sunday, March 24, 1929, about Smith found guilty of murder on retrial. Few people in the county saw the paper, but they already knew that the Banks County Superior Court had convicted Wash Smith of murder for the second time for the slaying of Jud Wells. The judge sentenced him to be electrocuted on May 3.

Wash thought he only had a month before the date the judge ordered. That would not give the lawyer much time to get what they needed to request for a third trial. His lawyer started the paperwork as soon as Wash left for Clark County. It relieved Wash that he had already started on the work. Wash knew that when the state scheduled an execution, the prisoner had to be in Milledgeville for at least two days before the scheduled date and not over two months. As it was, he only had one month before the execution, and he was told the state would transfer him to the State penitentiary in Milledgeville.

The lawyer was busy getting information together for Wash's case to request another trial. He was finding out that there were more issues with the case than he could have expected. When he went to get information about why Billie Joe Brown and why the sheriff could not find her, no one wanted to talk about it. After checking with several people in the community that knew her, it was becoming clear that they would not tell what they knew because of pressure from someone. The lawyer had his suspicions about who was pressuring everybody, but he did not want to jeopardize himself or his case by digging too much into the matter. It was becoming clear to Wash's lawyer that a lot more influential individuals in the county were around, making it hard for him to get the evidence, he needed to help get a fair trial.

Every day Wash expected to be told to pack his things and leave for Milledgeville. Every day he did not go was a relief. Days passed, weeks passed, and months passed, and nothing was ever said about packing to move. It put stress on his mind and body, not knowing when that dreadful day would come. So many times, he was ready to give up, but he carried on. The visits he got from the Evangelical Businessmen's Club were some he treasured. They conducted Bible studies and led the singing of the hymns he grew up hearing at his home church.

***

September 12, 1929

Not a lot of news came from home over the next several months. Wash only got an occasional telegram or would find a news article in one newspaper. Both telegrams and news articles only gave a very brief summary of what was happening. The telegrams he got were short because it cost money for each word sent, so the messages from home had to be short. He decided that the newspaper only went into details about him when it was reporting about events that created him as a hardened criminal.

In the latest telegram, Wash learned that Sue Smith had passed away on September 11, 1928, about two in the morning. He had not heard that there was anything the matter with her, and he was sad to hear about her passing. Reading the telegram brought back memories of everybody back home. He wondered about Daisy, Horace, and Curtis. It hurt him that his friends did not testify for him during his trial, but he could not hate them for what they did. With three young children at home, Wash wondered what happened to them and where they would live. He guessed they did like all the other tenants on the farm and continued living where they were. The family had lived there for some time, and there was no need to push them out of the house to let another struggling family move in. The brothers and sisters were old enough to continue like they had in the past and work and take care of their family. Sue had taught them that.

There seemed to be a lot of confusion in the cell for the last several days. Wash felt like something was about to happen, but he could not exactly figure it out. Several of the prisoners gathered in the back of the cell and discussed things in a low whisper. He did not think it was any of his concern. If there was going to be trouble, he needed no more at this time to deal with. Wash stayed to himself and never tried to get in other people's business. One afternoon there was something strange happening. It was the last week in October and there was an escape at the Clark County Jail, and four prisoners pried open a ventilator and fled. They tried to get Wash to leave with them, but Wash thought that the escape would hurt his chances of a lighter sentence. The officers captured the escapees shortly afterward. Wash thought it would have been a disaster to have gone and breathed a sigh of relief that he did not go.

To pass time, Wash wrote a letter to the newspaper to let his family and friends know how he was doing. Wash wrote:

November 11, 1929

Letter from Wash Smith

Dear Editor: Will ask you to spare me a place in your paper to say a few words. I am in Athens Jail awaiting hearing from Supreme Court after being kept a prisoner two years charged with the murder of Jud Wells and I think the lord will take care of me. I was held a prisoner here for five months. There were nine prisoners trying to escape. They broke jail and were about to make their getaway, and I remained in my cell. The jailer asked me why I didn't go too. I told him that I was trusting in the Lord to take care of me and give me justice and then I will be satisfied. I want the good old people of Banks County to know I am not in sorrow so much. It will be surprising for some of the people to know that I think enough of my county to write them a word and I had a wonderful dream here in Clark County jail. I dreamed that I come clear of the charge they have got me for and was the pastor of the old Mountain View church and I pray every night that my dream will come true, and I can surely say that I have had dreams to come to pass and many prayers answered since I have been in prison. So I hope and trust to the Lord that this one will be answered and I want to thank the good people that are holding to me through thick and thin, for if anyone would stop to think how it would be if they were in my place then they could have some sympathy for me. I sure hope that they will never be in my place unjustified for there is not no pleasure in it, but I am praying to the Lord that I will get justice in my case before it is too late. Well, I will bring this to a close for this time, and if this time and if this hits the waste basket, I will come again. If you will print this for me, I sure will be glad about it.

Very Truly yours,

WASH SMITH

***

When the paper printed his letter, family members made sure they got a copy of the paper. The article joined the other ones his loved ones had clipped and saved in the envelopes they placed in Bibles or old trunks.

Visits from home became scarce while Wash was in Athens. The few times he was back in Homer, he could always count on seeing some of his family or friends. Wash looked forward to any visit. In Athens, he did not expect to see anyone often, but he looked forward to getting telegrams from his brother, who worked on the railroad in South Carolina. His brother Edward kept him informed with the news from around the home. He told him how his mother and grandfather were. He was especially eager to hear about his mother and relieved to find out she was well. Edward was a good brother to Wash. He did what he could to help him and their mother. They did not expect Wash to send them a telegram. Wash saved all that he received so he could read over again when his thoughts took him back to the old home place.

The last telegram Wash received from his brother upset him. Edward told Wash that there was some interference by the prosecution and by Jud's family. He said there was pressure put on Billie Joe about her testimony. They were not sure what happened, but locating her and getting her to come to court as a witness for the defense was not working out. Wash's lawyer could not establish the details about why it was such a problem finding her to come to testify. Wash also found out that a juror had made a statement against Wash before the trial started that could have prejudiced the jury. He found out there was a lot of talk around the community about what the juror said and who made the comment. Mr. Early Stark and Jas. W. Adams were the defense attorneys for Wash and were working to get answers to both issues.

Wash had a hard time sleeping that night after getting the telegram. He tossed and turned on his prison cot, trying to make sense out of the news from home. He was finding it hard to believe that his friends turned a cold shoulder toward him, or an indifferent one. They knew what the sentence would be. Wash kept telling himself that it was self-defense. He was believing what he thought several months ago about things not adding up was possibly true. The situation looked like a catastrophe for Wash at the time if the courts did not grant a retrial in March or if the Governor would grant clemency if the court did not grant a new trial.

All Wash could do was wait. He had to wait for the lawyers to file papers for a retrial, for more telegrams from home that would tell if someone would come to his defense, and for the Governor to give him clemency if that was even a possibility. Wash was praying for help from above. He remembered what the Businessmen's Club in Athens had said one time during a visit. The verse had something to do with asking. Wash tried to find the verse in the New Testament Bible the men gave him several weeks ago. He knew it had to be in there somewhere because he remembered following along in his Bible as one man read the verses he was trying to locate. Wash thumbed through the pages, searching off and on all evening. He finally fell asleep trying to locate the verse.

The next morning, Wash woke up and tried to think of more of the verse. He knew it went something like ask and you will get or something like that. Wash spent hours looking for the verse and finding comfort in what he was reading. He looked forward to the Men's Club coming again and had a lot of questions for them to answer. Wash was determined to find that verse, and not exactly knowing the words seemed to give him some hope because of his situation. He tried to find out from some of the prison guards if they knew when the Men's Club would come back. After several days, one guard came by the cell to tell the prisoners the Club would come that afternoon. That was good news to Wash, and he seemed to be more at ease after hearing of their pending visit that day.

The Evangelical Men's Club came after the jail had given the prisoners their afternoon meal. Wash had his Bible out and ready for them when they arrived. After the usual greeting and a brief prayer with each prisoner, one man led a short Bible study. He told those that were at the meeting to turn their Bibles to Matthew six, beginning with verse nine. He read verse nine, "After this manner, therefore, pray: Our Father which art in heaven, Hallowed be thy name."

They kept reading the Lord's Prayer and Wash knew all the words. He learned it when he was little and it just stuck in his mind. He caught himself saying the words along with them. When they got to the end, he said along with them out loud, "Forever, Amen."

Wash followed along with the reading, and this time he listened carefully to every word. The prisoners were told this is how Jesus taught us how to pray. He went through each line, telling the prisoners what it meant. It gave Wash a lot to think about. When the group was getting ready to leave, Wash stopped one man to ask if he could help him find a verse he had been looking for in his Bible. Several heard Wash ask and all of them were glad to see that he was opening up more to their lessons. Wash asked if he remembered the verse that was read several weeks ago about asking and getting. The man knew the verse that Wash was referring to and told him to read Matthew Chapter seven. When the men left, Wash sat on his cot and turned his little Bible to the chapter the man told him to read.

Wash did not have too much trouble finding the verse since Matthew was the first book in his Bible. He sat quietly and read silently, "Matthew Chapter seven verse seven: Ask, and it shall be given you; seek, and ye shall find; knock, and it shall be opened unto you. "

Wash had been seeking that chapter. He put a piece of paper to mark where it was so he could turn right to the verse when he needed comforting. He did not know what all the words meant, but verses seven and eight were what he remembered. His friends and family had let him down a lot of times from what he had asked them. So, he knew this was not referring to them but to a Higher Being.

CHAPTER 17:
DENIED AGAIN

Thursday, February 27, 1930

Wash got news from his lawyer that they had denied a retrial in the March 1930 term of the Superior Court in Banks County. There had been additional evidence relating to the case that possibly proved that the shooting was in self-defense and that a juror had expressed an opinion before the trial that would have disqualified him from serving on the case. On February 27, 1930, they had refused the condemned slayer a new trial. Wash saw an article about the shooting that was said to have arisen out of attention paid by Smith to the daughter of the merchant. He did not understand how the newspaper got that wrong. Wash was not seeing his daughter. It was Sue's daughter. The defense appealed the case because the trial court declined to postpone the case. After all, the state hid a witness and was not present for the trial. It also appealed because one juror had expressed an opinion in the case before the trial. The evidence proved neither, the Supreme Court determined, and it denied the trial.

Wash found out that his lawyer had filed an extraordinary motion for a new trial on Wash's behalf. After the trial, during the March term of 1929, there were at least two irregularities during the trial that needed to be addressed. Mr. Stark explained that an extraordinary motion for a new trial allows the defendant to dispute a conviction based upon newly discovered evidence. They can file it after the conviction. Once Mr. Stark filed all the paperwork for the request for a retrial, things happened quickly in the court system. Wash thought that since they had denied his request for a retrial, this motion would be his only chance of showing that there was additional evidence. What he found out, besides recent evidence, was that his last two trials were not as impartial as he had hoped they should have been. He had put all his trust in the court system to make sure that his trial was fair and just.

The lawyer stated the grounds outlined in Wash's motion for a new trial was that Billie Joe Brown was a material witness for the defense. The prosecution kept her from appearing at the court. When the defense tried to issue a subpoena to the only witness who could testify on Wash's behalf, the prosecution and the Wells family kidnapped her, maliciously and feloniously, with the sole purpose of depriving her to testify for Wash. They kept Billie Joe Brown out of the way of the officers, preventing them from serving her the subpoena and keeping her from coming to court and giving testimony on behalf of the defendant. The lawyer presented in the motion for a new trial that the prosecution had kept the witness from attending court. The sheriff could not issue a subpoena to her. Although the courts had issued a subpoena regularly for her and an officer dispatched to her home to serve the subpoena, the prosecution had taken charge of Billie Joe Brown and hid her from the officer by keeping her in a closet, and running her from one house to another and keeping her away from the officers with the subpoena until the trial was over.

Billie Joe had told the threats Jud made to Wash, and she was the only witness who could swear to the relevant facts to Wash's primary defense. Billie Joe Brown sent an affidavit stating that she would testify to the fact that Jud Wells had threatened the life of Wash Smith and that she had told Wash of the threat Jud made to him. Billie Joe had told Wash about the threat before the day of the shooting. Wash's lawyer, Mr. Stark, said that Billie Joe was the only material witness who could prove the facts that Jud threatened Wash.

The authorities attached a copy of the affidavits of Billie Joe Brown, now Billie Joe Stewart, stating the alleged facts as exhibit "A" and made a part of this motion to Georgia, Banks County.

Personally, before me came Billie Joe Brown, who on oath says that she personally knows Wash Smith and that she knew Jud Wells in his lifetime. That on or about Tuesday or Wednesday before the trial of Wash Smith, I was at the home of my brother in the old Ruff Moses Home place in Banks County when the Sheriff's son come there to serve me with a subpoena to attend court as a witness for Wash Smith, and Felton Presley had told me not to let anybody see me or serve me with any paper to go to court, and when the officer come I got in a closet like I was told, and after the officer left, Felton Presley carried me to Cornelia to the home of R. C. Moses and I stayed there till Monday night, and June Presley came there and told me they did not have enough bed room there and I stopped at Felton Presleys on Monday night, and stayed there till Wednesday morning, and I then went back to R. C. Moses home and stayed there till Wednesday morning, and I then went back to R. C. Moses home and stayed there till Monday night, and the Sheriff's son or some officer come there to Mr. Moses home to serve me with a subpoena Wednesday and they would not let him in the house, or me see him and that night (Wednesday night) they carried me to a Mrs. Hermes and I stayed there one night, and one day, then Julia Presley come and told me the trial was over and I went back up to June Presleys and stayed till Saturday, and then Merle Moses brought me home.

I would have gone to court if I had a chance and told the truth. I would have sworn that I heard Jud Wells threaten the life of Wash Smith and that Wash Smith was told it, and that he threatened to kill him about Daisy Smith.

It made this affidavit to be used as evidence in the motion for a new trial in the case of the State VS Wash Smith on May seventeenth, before Hon. W. W. Stark or at such time and place as he may direct.

It relieved Wash that there was something in writing from Billie Joe that would prove he was not making things up. It also relieved him that an affidavit was now part of the case and the judge would grant a retrial. Wash felt better about how things were moving at this point. There had been so many disappointments in the last year that this had to help.

On the day of the hearing for a motion for a new trial, the prosecution said in its counter-argument that introducing the evidence as an affidavit of the witness, Billie Joe Brown, where she repudiated the material in the affidavit she offered to the defense. Honorable W. W. Stark, judge for Wash's case, said that under the law in such cases being tried, it was humanly impossible to determine if the affidavit of Billie Joe Brown to be the truth, and cannot consider her affidavit as evidence. The prosecution said that the force and effect of the affidavit offered to the defense were annulled and voided in effect by a repudiated affidavit filed by the prosecution.

Wash nor Mr. Stark did not know that the affidavit filed was a forgery until about the twenty-fifth day of March 1930. They learned that Billie Joe Brown did not sign the affidavit, nor did anyone authorized by her to do so. The forgery of Billie Joe's affidavit was the defendant's principal weapon of defense and that this forgery deprived Wash of proving that Jud Wells had threatened to take his life. It was the general opinion was that if she could testify, the court would grant a new trial for Wash and her evidence could have probably resulted in a different verdict in the case. The defense also discovered that the prosecution had forged Billie Joe's name on the affidavit to void all material facts in her affidavit offered to the defense on the motion for a new trial. Mr. Stark filed an Extraordinary Motion for a new trial stating that the state and prosecution had deprived and defrauded Wash of a fair and impartial trial that the laws and constitution of Georgia entitled him to have.

Besides the fraudulent affidavit mentioned in the extraordinary motion, it stated that one juror had formed and expressed an opinion against Wash. The court should sanction the motion and grant a new trial to him, because of one juror, L. J. Bennett had made the comment against the defendant before his selection and qualification as a juror. His remark should have disqualified him for an appointment and as foreman of the jury. The statement about Wash could have interfered with him receiving a fair trial. Mr. Bennett based his comment on what he had heard during the first trial in 1928. He had formed and expressed his opinion from the first trial and commented to W. O. Arnold, a citizen of Banks County, less than one hour from the time Bennett took the oath of a juror and qualified in the case.

Mr. Bennett expressed his opinion saying, "Bill, do you know that we have got one of the worst criminals to try here that Banks County has ever had, and that is Wash Smith, and if I was on the jury, I would send him to the electric chair."

That remark should have disqualified Bennett as a juror on the grounds of him forming and expressing his opinion during the retrial of 1929. It should have disqualified him on the grounds of being prejudiced and biased against the defendant before and at the time they selected and qualified him as a juror. It should have also disqualified Mr. Arnold as being unfit to serve as a juror for being influenced by the opinions of prejudice and bias of Mr. Bennett against Wash. Bennett's statement made it impossible for Wash to have a fair and impartial trial which the constitution and laws of the state of Georgia accorded him. The language he expressed against Wash before the trial clearly showed that Mr. Bennett was more partial to the state and against the accused.

For the court to appoint L. J. Bennett as foreman of the jury and for the court to know that he showed partiality toward the state and against Wash, the court should have removed Bennett from the jury. Bennett had formed a prejudiced and biased opinion against Wash before the trial, all based on what Mr. Bennett heard in the first trial. That made it impossible for the court to render a fair and impartial trial to Wash the constitution allowed to him by law. His appointment as foreman placed a great weight against the defendant. Billie Joe Brown and L. J. Bennett had copies of supporting affidavits attached to be part of the extraordinary motion required by law in such cases. The court should sanction the extraordinary motion for a new trial. Early Stark and Jas. W. Adams, attorneys for Wash, filed a rule nisi directed to the Honorable Clifford Platt, solicitor general for the state, requiring him to show cause before this court that a rule is absolute and a new trial granted. The two lawyers filed a supersedes to make a stay of execution of the sentence until the courts could hear and dispose of the motion for a retrial. The lawyer filed this on the thirty-first day of March 1930 while the March term of the Banks Superior Court was still open.

W. O. Arnold went to George T. Buffett, a notary public, to make a statement for the court about what had happened just before the March 1929 retrial of Wash

Smith. Mr. Arnold said that as the jury was being selected he owned a restaurant in the town of Homer and about noon on the day of the selection Mr. L. J. Bennett came to his place and asked about getting his dinner on credit. Mr. Bennett said, "Do you know we have got one of the worst criminals on trial we ever had in this county, and that Wash Smith was the worst criminal in the county. Mr. Bennett said that if he was on the jury, he would send him to the electric chair."

Mr. Arnold made this affidavit for it being used before the Prison Commission of Georgia and the Governor of Georgia, and before any other body in the hearing of this motion. He signed the paper and Mr. Buffett notarized it for the lawyers to present with the paperwork to be presented to the commission and the Governor. Mr. John Hill and Mr. Nolan Hill went before the clerk of Superior Court Theodore Cheek to swear to the good character of W. O. Arnold to support the motion for a new trial for Wash.

Mr. Arnold stated that on March 30th, 1930 Jas. W. Adams and Early Stark came to his home and asked if he had heard what L. J. Bennett said that if he was on the jury that he would electrocute Wash Smith, and Mr. Arnold said he did. The two lawyers asked Arnold if he would go to Bennett's home and face him in the matter. Mr. Adams went in and asked if Bennett made the comment and Bennett said, "That he said every word of it." Adams asked if he really felt that way in his heart when he said it to Mr. Arnold, and Bennett replied, "That he certainly did."

Bennett said, "I am going to stick to my convictions, and no man can change me. That fellow, meaning Wash Smith, broke up a good family and he ought to have been in the ground long ago. I feel we ought to take our shotguns and go get him and settle it that way." He turned to Mr. Arnold and said, "Don't you think so, Bill?"

After the visit, the two lawyers felt that the evidence to get a new trial would insure one would be granted. Mr. Adams wrote an affidavit to be added to the others. Much of his affidavit was the same as Arnold's, but Bennett said further, "I am going to stick to my convictions, that fellow, meaning Smith, broke up a good family, and he ought to have been in the ground long ago. I feel we ought to take our shotguns and go get him and settle that way, and turned to Arnold and said, don't you think so Bill, to which Arnold replied, "I want shooting to be the last thing I have to do."

Mr. Adams says that he never in his life met someone with so much feeling against a man as Mr. Bennett showed he had against Wash Smith. They made this affidavit to be used in the hearing of the extraordinary motion for a new trial in the state's case vs Wash Smith after the 1929 trial.

Wash was back to feeling down and out about his trial. It was looking as if everybody at home did not support him. The influence and pressure of the Wells brothers had put everybody that Wash thought were his friends against him. His lawyer said it was in his best interest to put the case before the prison commission and the Governor. Surely, there he could get justice.

Things in the court system seemed to move fast since February. Lawyers filed motions for retrials when recent evidence showed up about the trial. Newspaper articles in The Atlanta Constitution started showing up every day or so. On Friday, March 28, the state prison commission had under consideration a petition asking the commission of his sentence. The judge sentenced Wash to die in the electric chair the next Wednesday, April 2nd, for the murder of Jud Wells. Wash was confident that they would spare his life. They had denied him a new trial by the Banks County superior court and later by the state supreme court.

Several days before March 28th, they put a petition containing names of several hundred Banks County citizens and from other counties before the Governor and then the prison commission as a last-minute effort to have the sentence commuted to life imprisonment. The defense claimed that the prosecuting attorneys and members of the Wells family "locked up" a young girl, Miss Billie Joe Brown, who was to be the defense's principal witness. When the sheriff came to serve subpoenas for the trial, they could not find her. Miss Brown, who lived on the Wells farm at the time of the shooting, had evidence that would probably have changed the verdicts of the juries in the trials had they allowed her to testify.

In an interview with the newspaper, Wash told the reporter, "I was working for Wells at his whisky distillery at the time of the shooting. The shotgun I shot him with was the gun I used to guard the stills with. He had thirteen men working at the stills and sold whisky by wholesale."

The reporter stated in the paper that the girl whom Mr. Smith intended to marry Miss Smith, but was only fourteen years old at the time of the shooting. She testified against Smith at the trials because of "high pressure" from the Wells family, according to Wash. She married another man some time ago.

The court held a hearing on an application for commutation of the sentence on Thursday, March 27th. The prison commission was taking the matter under advisement. Wash would expect any decision before Monday or Tuesday of the next week. The state had scheduled Wash to be electrocuted on that Tuesday. He now felt that his destiny was in the hands of the prison commission and the governor. He did not think that his lawyers would do anything at this point and told the sheriff that was with him something had to happen by Tuesday. The sheriff could tell in Wash's face that he was extremely worried about his future.

The sheriff told Wash that he needed to get his things together for a move to the State Penitentiary in Milledgeville. He had to be in the penitentiary two days before the scheduled sentence. So the move had to be done immediately to get Wash there by Sunday. The sudden move to Milledgeville was very upsetting to Wash, and the sheriff tried his best to comfort Wash's emotions. At the penitentiary, they processed Wash into the institution for the electric chair, and they placed him in the death cell. The sheriff from home stood guard.

Chaplain Edwin Atkins came by to see Wash and let him know if he needed to talk to him, to let him know. Chaplain Atkins was the prison chaplain at the State Institution where it held prisoners convicted of the death penalty. He preached sermons to the convicts and prayed with the inmates before their execution. He dedicated himself to making sure the prisoner heard about salvation and kept a journal of all the men that came through Milledgeville Prison. Wash had got to the institution just days before the time they scheduled him for the electric chair. It was important for the chaplain that he talked with Wash about his salvation. He prayed often for Wash.

The chaplain knew time was important for Wash. He sat with him for a long time that first evening. Wash was at his cell talking to the chaplain about what he believed. It relieved Chaplain Atkins when he heard that the Athens Evangelical Businessmen's Club had made an impression on Wash. Even though Atkins knew nothing about the group in Athens, he could tell that their influence on Wash had made a significant difference. Wash told Atkins that he had struggled a lot with his belief. This he told the chaplain when he first met the Athens Businessmen's Club. He said little to them and only listened. As time went on, Wash told them he believed he was too far gone with all the things he had done to have a place in Heaven. Wash told the Chaplain that the Men gave him a Bible, and he started reading the scriptures they shared with Wash. He said after a while he had a lot of questions for the Men's Club about those scriptures. It deeply moved Chaplain Atkins to see that Wash was relating to him.

Reverend Atkins was always concerned about the souls of these prisoners. He knew they all had made choices in life that got them to that point. He said not one person is good, as in Romans 3:10, "As it is written. There is none righteous, no, not one." He would tell them everybody had sinned and that his God was a forgiving God no matter what they had done. He would forgive them. Atkins would read Romans 3:23, "For all have sinned, and come short of the glory of God." Sin came from man and in Romans 5:12, "Wherefore, as by one man sin entered into the world, and death by sin, and so death passes upon all men, for that all have sinned." Romans 6: 23, "For the wages of sin is death; but the gift of God is eternal life through Jesus Christ our Lord." tells us God's price for sin. Reverend Atkins said that Paul tells us our way out is in Romans 5:8, But God commendeth His love toward us, in that, while we were yet sinners, Christ died for us." Reverend Atkins turned his Bible to Romans 10:13 and handed it to Wash. Wash read the scripture aloud, "For whosoever shall call upon the name of the Lord shall be saved." Chaplain Atkins turned his Bible to Romans 10: 9 and 10 and read to Wash, "That if thou shalt confess with thy mouth the Lord Jesus, and shalt believe in thine heart that God hath raised him from the dead, thou shalt be saved. For with the heart, man believeth unto righteousness; and with the mouth, confession is made unto salvation." The chaplain quoted John 3:16, "For God so loved the world that he gave his only begotten Son, that whosoever believeth in him should not perish, but have everlasting life." He said that the entire Bible is summed up in one sentence. Mr. Atkins reassured Wash that all a person had to do was to admit that they are a sinner and need to be saved. Atkins added that all a person needs to do is to believe that Christ died for you on the cross of Calvary. Wash needed the promise that Chaplain Atkins was showing him in the Bible.

Wash had read these verses before in his cell in Athens; he knew what these words meant. He did not tell the Businessmen's Club that he understood what it took for him to go to Heaven. Wash thought back to that day and remembered burying his face in his pillow and weeping. He knew he needed to do something before it was too late, but he was not sure if he had assured his place in Heaven. Atkins read John 14:6, "Jesus saith unto him, I am the way, the truth, and the life: no man cometh unto the Father, but by me." He read John 5:24, "Verily, verily, I say unto you, He that hear my word, and believeth on him that sent me, hath everlasting life, and shall not come into condemnation; but is passed from death unto life." Followed by Hebrews 9:27, he read aloud, "And as it is appointed unto men once to die, but after this the judgment:" That last verse hit Wash deeply. He looked at Chaplain Atkins with tears streaming down his face and said, "That is tomorrow. That will be my once to die."

Wash struggled to get the words out so the chaplain could understand what he was saying because they kept sticking in his throat. Wash fell to his knees, and Chaplain Atkins put his hand on his shoulder for comfort and reassurance. Chaplain Atkins heard Wash say, "Dear Lord Jesus, I know that I am a sinner. I know that I need you. I believe that you died on the cross for me. Forgive me of my sins. Right now, I turn from my sins and open the door of my heart and life to you. I receive you as my Savior. Come into my life and save me. Thank you for what you did on the cross for me. Amen." The chaplain shook Wash's hand and could see a difference in him. It relieved Atkins that Wash had made a decision so important to him.

The news report from an Atlanta paper had another article on April the first. The state prison commission would prepare to act on the petition of Wash Smith that was presented to them last week. It summarized the events that an argument involving a girl brought about the shooting. They tried last week to take the case before Governor L. G. Hardman. Wash found out that Governor Hardman was from Commerce, Georgia. Wash did not know if the Governor knew any of the people involved in his case, since almost everybody involved came from either Homer or Commerce. The Governor declined to consider it until the prison commission had heard the appeal for clemency. Wash thought that did not give any time for the Governor to consider the case.

Wash went to bed that night, unsure of his destiny on the next day. That was the worst night Wash had in about two years when this ordeal all started. Before he left Banks County Jail in March, his lawyer explained to him the purpose of the extraordinary motion for a new trial. The lawyer presented the additional evidence and submitted the petition to the prison commission and Governor. He was in Athens only a few days before the sheriff took Wash to Milledgeville. It was less than 24 hours before Wash was to meet death in the electric chair when the Georgia Supreme Court issued an order staying the execution pending an appeal of an extraordinary motion for a new trial. The order interrupted deliberations of the state prison commission on a last-minute appeal for clemency. A court official held up the execution at least until July when the Supreme Court could hear the appeal in the regular order of business. It relieved Wash at the news that the Georgia Supreme Court issued the stay of execution.

They issued the order on the stay of the execution on an application for a mandamus to compel Judge W. W. Stark, of Commerce, to issue a supersedes staying the execution pending the appeal of the extraordinary motion for the new trial which Judge Stark refused. Wash did not know what these legal terms meant, but later on, learned that a higher court issued a mandamus to compel an action of a lower court to request an order to stop the proceedings. He only knew it delayed the execution until the prison commission or the Governor decided, hopefully in Wash's favor. A supersedes, Wash learned, was to suspend the authority of a trial court to issue an execution of a judgment that they had appealed on Wash's behalf. Judge Stark did not want to stop the execution of his judgment because of pressure from the Wells family. So, the higher court ordered the lower court to enforce the stay of execution until the appeals court had time to review the appeal.

The Superior Court Judge, Stark, denied the motion yesterday, and he signed the bill of exceptions. The bill of exception is used to explain the circumstances and the evidence regarding the objection. In the absence of a supersedes, the execution that was set for this morning would have been carried out before the Supreme Court reviewed the questions presented. The Supreme Court acted on it "to preserve jurisdiction" pending the hearing. Wash felt better to find out that the Supreme Court was overruling Judge Stark's orders since it looked like he was acting in the best interest of the Wells family instead of Wash. He thought it was no wonder he was having trouble proving his claim of self-defense. Wash was more confident that his hope would be in the Governor's decision to issue clemency.

Wash's lawyer Early C. Stark said they based the motion for a new trial primarily on evidence submitted to the prison board. This happened last Tuesday during the hearing's course. The motion stated that one juror had stated before being chosen that he would "break that fellow's neck," referring to Wash. The motion also alleged the fact that the prosecution had "hid out," the chief defense witness, Billie Joe Brown.

Wash also found out that a delegation representing the Athens Businessmen's Evangelical Club appeared before the prison commission to plead for clemency. They dismissed the hearing before the prison board on the announcement of the action of the Supreme Court. The prison board is considered primarily as a body of last resort for a condemned prisoner. After that development, they took Wash from Milledgeville and moved back to Athens to remain in jail there pending recent development in the case.

A sigh of relief came over Wash. He thought the recent development was a good sign of justice for his case. That had been a quick trip down and back from Milledgeville, and Wash learned that the trials he had in Banks County may have been more of a formality toward him being found guilty than a trial to find the truth and rule self-defense.

The month of April passed slowly for Wash. Fortunately for Wash, they delayed execution until at least July. Wash looked for telegrams and messages from his lawyer to find out the developments in his case. The Athens Jail got The Atlanta Constitution daily, so he could search through each issue for articles about his hearing.

CHAPTER 18: FOLLOWING THE NEWS

Wednesday, April 30, 1930

At the end of April, he read that the Clark County officers were looking for five prisoners who escaped the jail earlier the day before through a ventilator door they pried open. The door led to the top of the jail, where they crossed the courthouse roof and slid down a garden hose to freedom. The five prisoners tried to persuade Wash and four other prisoners to join them in the escape, but they all declined to take advantage of the opportunity to escape.

Wash notified the bailiff, H. D. Duff of the escape, shortly before 6 a.m. and the search started immediately. This was the second time since Wash had been under the death sentence that he refused to escape. Both times the escapees had pried the ventilator door open to allow the prisoners to leave.

***

Tuesday, October 21, 1930

Wash did not get a lot of information from his lawyers or from telegrams from home between April 1930 and October 1930. He sat in his cell and thought about his life back home. He remembered back in 1918 when he was nine years old and many in the community became very sick from the flu. Wash was young and strong and avoided the sickness. It may have been to his advantage that he was outside as much as he was. Schools were closed across the state, but in the rural counties of the area, the schools were closed for other reasons. That fall in September seemed to be the start of that flu season, but most of the children were out of school anyway to help with the harvesting of the crops the family had planted in the spring. Farmers were planting fall and winter crops like turnips, collards, and cabbage. They cut and gathered hay to put in the barn for the animals to eat over the winter. Wash thought that life was busy and took a lot of work to keep things going. He longed for those days again.

He got some very disturbing news on Tuesday, October twenty-first, that the Georgia Supreme Court yesterday upheld the death sentence of Wash following a second conviction and appeal. Smith claimed in his first appeal that persons interested in him being prosecuted had illegally detained a material witness in his case and the high court ordered a new trial. The Georgia Supreme Court found no error in the second trial and would not change the verdict from the two trials. Wash got word that he would move from Athens. The authorities said he was going to be moved for safekeeping. The sheriff took Wash from Athens and moved him to Fulton County

***

Thursday: November 6, 1930

They transferred Wash to the Fulton County Jail on Thursday, November 6. As the sheriff was taking Wash from the car, he saw an opening for a quick getaway. Without thinking, he fled. A low-hung cable in the yard of the Atlanta Milling Company tripped him, and they recaptured him before he could scramble to his feet. He attempted outside the front door of The Tower Thursday night. Wash did not know why he ran. Shortly afterward, the guards securely confined him to his cell in Fulton County Jail

One of the local newspapers reported he had tried to escape.. That transfer was one he did not like. The buildings were large and dull-looking. Inside was loud and smelled. The looks from the outside gave him an eerie feeling, with the tall circular tower high above the building and the stained bricks caused by age. Wash found out that because of the tall round guard tower on the corner of the jail, people commonly called the Fulton County Jail "The Tower."

He remembered that a few months ago he passed up an opportunity to make his getaway from the Clarke County jail at Athens. Wash told the warden that he could have escaped too, but he refused to make the break. He did not want to hurt his chances of clemency. Suddenly, he felt desperate and ran. After that last bit of news in October that Wash got from the Supreme Court about them upholding the verdict of the death sentence, he did not see that there would be any hope of getting a lesser sentence. The only thing left for Wash was the Prison Commission and the Governor. He hoped that the last two would be a different verdict and not the same as those before. He continued to hope for clemency and did not think that outside forces would sway the commission or the Governor.

***

Monday, November 10, 1930

There seemed to be a lot of interest in Wash for the newspapers to keep putting articles about him. Wash usually read over the paper to find out about what was going on around the area. Finally, they informed Wash that the state prison commission would give a final hearing on Wednesday on an application for commutation. Hopefully, on Wednesday, he would know if they would commute his sentence to life in prison. He had thoughts that made him think that all of this had been a wasted effort for him to hope for self-defense, but he did not want to give up hope either.

***

Wednesday, November 12, 1930

A report from one of the newspapers in Milledgeville stated that Wash's lawyer Stark had filed an affidavit with the prison commission that was signed by Oliver Brock. Mr. Stark asked for a commutation of the death sentence to life imprisonment. According to his lawyer, Brock is the only living eyewitness to the shooting of Jud Wells.

Oliver, with three other men, went to Mr. Stark's home Sunday night. Stark related how Brock had sworn falsely against Smith.

Mr. Stark said, "It had so weighed on his conscience that he had to tell the truth, and he told it regardless of the fact that it probably will send him back to the Ohio penitentiary."

He had been paroled from an Ohio prison and placed in the custody of an uncle of Jud Wells. Oliver knew denial of his testimony would probably mean his return to prison but was determined to clear his conscience.

During the trials, Stark said, Brock testified Wells was slain by Smith without provocation. His repudiation affidavit said the men quarreled, and Smith seized a shotgun and fired after Wells had reached under the counter.

Mr. Stark also said that he had been informed that Will Freeman, the other eyewitness, died recently of typhoid fever. He had repudiated his testimony on his deathbed.

Wash's first thought was that, finally, someone had come to help him. He could not understand what had changed Oliver's mind to help him, but it relieved him that someone from home had come to his rescue. That bit of news gave him hope that there could be an appeal for a lesser sentence.

Attorney J. B. Hogan of Banks County, who aided the state in the prosecution, appeared before the commission and told the commissioners he had investigated the report that Freeman had repudiated his testimony and there appeared to be no basis for the report. Clifford Pratt, solicitor general of Banks superior court, requested that no commutation of the sentence be recommended.

***

Thursday, November 13, 1930

Wednesday's news was not what Wash had hoped to hear about his case. His heart raced after hearing his plea was being delayed. The delay was heartbreaking. Wash knew that the Georgia Prison Commission had taken under consideration clemency appeals for him. Many times, he got good news from reading the paper, but it only brought him doom. Wash looked at the calendar and could just glance at it to see there was not much time left. He was to be electrocuted a week from Saturday. He had not expected to be that close to that date.

Ten days was not very many days for another appeal. All he had left was the Governor. A sentence in an article that he had read said, "A week from Saturday." Those four words kept echoing in his mind way into the night.

Friday, November 14, 1930

Wash Smith

 Things could only get worse for Wash. He read in the paper that the prison board refused a plea for mercy and knew the Governor would not make any kind of decision on the plea until the prison board had made their recommendation. Governor Hardman was the only hope remaining for Wash not to be sentenced to the chair. The Governor requested that Wash's fingerprints be taken and an alienist to evaluate Wash to determine his mental and character tendencies before he made his decision on Wash's fate. The alienist evaluation was at The Tower, and Carl I. Sherwood evaluation was not received in time for the Governor to use in his evaluation for his fingerprints to determine his character

If Governor Hardman did not intervene with the sentencing, they would electrocute Wash on November 22. The state prison commission acted on Thursday about his plea and declined to recommend clemency.

Wash was still in the Fulton Tower and still hopeful of executive action to save his life. Wash repeated a statement that he had made many times before that he shot Jud following a quarrel over the girl he was engaged to marry. While Wash was repeating his trial plea for self-defense, Jud's brother was in Fulton Tower talking to the warden and guards at the jail for the sole purpose of seeing that Smith did not escape. After a visit to the jail, his brother said he was going to the state capitol to see that nothing saved Wash from the chair.

Wash heard that Jud's brother had been at the jail from prisoners and guards but could not believe that Jud's brother boldly made a statement that he wanted nothing to stop the sentence. Wash thought it would be eight days until that dreadful time. Surely, with Oliver's statement, the Governor would see that it is self-defense.

***

Saturday, November 15, 1930

Wash read yesterday's paper that Jud's brother made a bold statement that there was to be nothing to stop the execution. Today, there was an article wanting the paper to correct a statement that Jud's brothers made and asked the paper Friday to correct a statement associated with the Wells brother Friday morning about the case. The older brother said that the paper misquoted him when he said that he was going to the state capitol to make sure nothing saved that boy from the chair. Wells said that what he said was that he declined a ride from Fulton Tower as he was going to stop at the capitol. While he was at the prison, he said nothing about going to do everything in his power to send the man who killed his brother to the electric chair.

Wash had gotten to believe that all the reports he had been reading in the paper were correct, especially what was in there yesterday. Now the Wells brothers were pressuring the newspapers to change the story that made them look as though they were cold-hearted. He had always thought that they pressured his friends not to support his claim. The brothers went to visit the prison commission, and it convinced Wash that they pressured them too. Could they pressure the Governor too? Wash wondered if it would be possible for them to have that much influence to control the highest office in the state. Wash knew he was running out of time, and he would soon find out.

Monday, November seventeenth, Wash got up and was told the sheriff from Banks County would escort him to Milledgeville. The Governor had not decided on Wash's case. Wash asked the sheriff if he had heard anything about the Governor commuting the sentence to life in prison. He and Wash had gone through the last two-and-a-half years together, and the sheriff had gotten to know a little more about Wash as time passed. The sheriff told Wash that he had sent a letter to the Governor with a worker on the railroad to ask for a lighter sentence. Wash thanked the sheriff, and it moved the sheriff that he did. The sheriff had heard nothing but told Wash that he was about to stay with him while he was at the institution. The sheriff did not go into any of the details about why he was staying down there with Wash. He could tell that Wash had enough on his mind for now and did not need to have one more thing to worry about. The sheriff felt sorry for him and could see he still felt there was still some hope of a lesser sentence. Wash told the sheriff that it was self-defense, and if that does not come out in time before they executed him, the church would fall from its foundation during his funeral if he was innocent of murder.

Once they arrived at Milledgeville, Wash knew the routine of being processed into the prison. He knew the routine since he had already been at the institution earlier in the year. Like always, the guards at the prison did a complete search of Wash and his possessions. The prison uniforms were all the same black and white stripes, so the different clothes did not matter. Once the institution completed all the paperwork for entry into Milledgeville, they placed him in the death cell. It was the same one he was in earlier in the year. The sheriff stood guard at the cell. Things had not changed. It was not long before the chaplain came by to check on Wash. Chaplain Atkins hoped that things had worked out for Wash to get clemency and receive a life sentence for his crime. Wash told the chaplain that his lawyers referred his case to the prison commission for a review, and they refused his plea for mercy, and it was in the hands of the Governor. Chaplain Atkins had already known what Wash was telling him because he had read it in Wash's charts that came from the Fulton Tower. Atkins said a brief prayer with Wash and told him he would come back to see him before they turned the lights off for the night.

Wash did not expect to hear from his family for a few days since they moved him without much notice. Lately, Wash was having trouble sleeping and only slept for short periods throughout the day and night. This had become his usual sleeping habit for the last two or three weeks.

***

Friday, November 21, 1930

On the day before the scheduled sentencing, Wash read a newspaper article that the Governor had heard his plea. Governor Hardman would decide today what Wash's fate would be, and Wash was sure the Governor would rule in favor of a lesser sentence. Wash heard that a disinterested railroad flagman, L. E. Welborn, and the only lawyer who had stuck with him throughout this long legal battle, begged Governor Hardman on Thursday to commute the death sentence of Wash Smith. Also, attending the three-hour meeting resisting the appeal was Pemberton Cooley, a former solicitor-general, and J. G. B. Hogan, Banks County attorney employed by Jud's family, who were there pressuring the Governor to oppose any extension of executive clemency. Jud's brothers sat through the hearing.

L. E. Welborn brought the Governor the message from Sheriff Whelchel on behalf of the condemned boy. Welborn said he did not know the boy personally, but that he had impressed him with his story and with the statement of Sheriff Whelchel, who was taking Wash to Milledgeville on the train. Sheriff Whelchel was the Banks County officer who had been with Wash for the past two years of struggle.

Governor Hardman, after the hearing, announced that he would decide that day. The prison board had already declined to recommend clemency.

***

Friday, November 21, 1930

Later that afternoon, Wash got word that the Governor had decided. Wash had been anxious all day, awaiting word from the Governor. It looked like his answer to his prayer would finally come. A three-hour plea was his last hope for executive clemency, and it looked like he made that plea in vain. That meant that Wash Smith would die Saturday in the state's electric chair at Milledgeville. Governor Hardman declined Friday to commute Wash's sentence to life imprisonment, even after the three-hour session in which the Governor reviewed the long legal battle, and his lawyer and friends made appeals for Wash's life.

The refusal of executive clemency was Wash's last hope of life. The prison board had previously denied clemency as had a jury in a second trial and now the Governor. Wash could not help but think that the Governor would continue to think about the evidence brought to him and would later change his mind, even if it was at the last minute. Wash could only pray for someone to intercede for him.

The night before the scheduled electrocution was to take place, the Salvation Army and Chaplain Atkins went by the cell for several hours to be with Wash. He was sitting quietly toward the back of his cell but always felt like there would be hope for the Governor to intervene and stop the execution. He stayed to himself, as the others were singing hymns softly as the time passed. They sang hymns Wash was familiar with, but he sat in his chair quietly. They sang "Blessed Assurance" and they finally could hear him singing softly in the back of the cell the words to the song. Wash sang, "Perfect submission, perfect delight, Visions of rapture now burst on my sight; Angels, descending, bring from above Echoes of mercy, whispers of love." Tears welled up in the eyes of the Chaplain, the Salvation Army, and the guard from home.

Wash knew that the only hope he had was intervention by a higher force. He kept up his hope that something would change. It was getting late and everyone had to leave for the night. Rev. E. C. Atkins and Ensign

Scoville of the Salvation Army had been with Smith for several hours before the execution. He told them, "If this is my time to go, I am ready to meet my Maker."

It was hard for the chaplain to leave. All alone, Wash sat in the chair with the darkness surrounding him. Chaplain Atkins was always concerned about the souls of those who had gotten to this point in their lives. He had talked with Wash frequently concerning his soul and the chaplain was sure He would lead him home. At home, his mother looked at the old mantel clock as it struck six. She wondered if the Governor had issued a stay of execution. She could hear a whippoorwill calling as the sun went down behind the barn, and chills came over her when she heard it calling. It reminded her of what her grandmother always said when she heard one. She would say somebody is going to die. Her grandmother said an old Indian tale forewarned of ill fortune, or the bird would linger outside the house of someone sick waiting for them to die to snatch their soul. She shivered at the thought and brushed off the omen.

***

Saturday, November 22, 1930

The next morning Wash could sleep as late as he wanted. Nobody disturbed him on his last day. He slept until 8:30. An officer brought him whatever he wanted for breakfast, and he seemed to take great pleasure in his meal. It was hard to tell what Wash was thinking. A short time later, Chaplin Atkins returned when it was time for Wash to go. He silently prayed that Wash would forgo this punishment if at all possible, but he prayed that if it must be let him pass quickly.

The time for the execution was to be at 10:55 a.m. They gave Wash a change of clothes and he dressed in what they provided and silently waited. He wore baggy black-and-white striped prison clothes. The chaplain and the guard from home were his only comfort. They did not leave his side. Before it was time to go, the chaplain prayed one last time with Wash, and he handed him a white rose. The sheriff, chaplain, and Wash slowly walked down the hall to the chamber. The sheriff thought that Wash looked tired and worn from the ordeal of the last two years. He had lost weight and did not look as fit as he did before. The chaplain thought to himself that Wash walked so calmly, as though he knew a call from the Governor would come any second. Time passed too quickly and no call came.

There was the warden of the prison, two electricians, the chaplain, a doctor, and the sheriff from home that had been with Wash for most of the two years attended. None of Wash's family attended the execution. He knew it would have been too much for any of them to handle. His mother, being ill, stayed at her home in Banks County.

He looked over at the audience and those observing. Those whom he did not know, he stopped long enough to speak to each and every one and asked them their name and where they lived. The group entered the room where the chair was. It was the most prominent feature in the chamber. They shaved his head and the calf on one leg. He calmly walked forward and mounted the platform of the death chair at 10:45, and sat in the large white wooden chair. Wash did not want any of Jud's family or friends to witness the electrocution. He said, "I don't want to provide any thrill for relatives of that man!"

The Electric Chair

He turned to Warden J. M. Burke, who was the official executioner, and his assistants, including the electricians, urged them to make sure they set the connections firm so there would be no problems with this process. He said, "You do a good job. I've got to die only once and as I have got to go now, I want a good job made of it and see that there are no short circuits in the equipment."

The electricians made their tests. "I am ready to die," said Smith. "I do not deny that I killed Wells, but I think that I was justified."

They bound Wash to the chair at the wrists, ankles, and waist." Wash called for Chaplain Atkins to come to the chair. He told him, "Give this to mother," and he placed a small picture in his hand. Chaplain Atkins looked and it was a picture of his mother.

The attendants placed a band around his head to cover his eyes and placed straps on one leg and one on the top of his head to carry the electricity through his body. He did not struggle. Chaplain Atkins's white rose was all he had in his hand. When the time came for the official to complete the circuit, Chaplain Atkins was praying. They gave the first shock to him at 10:55 a.m. He was shaking involuntarily from the top of his head all the way down to his feet, and he quivered, twitched, and palpitated.

His hand clenched tightly onto the rose. Suddenly, Wash dropped the white rose when his hand relaxed and it fell to the floor. After another shock, they pronounced him dead at 11:05 a.m. and it was over. It was always hard for Chaplain Atkins when an execution was taking place. He viewed the prisoner in a different light than the prison officials did. He had gotten to know his inner feelings, and it saddened him greatly after each passing. The sheriff from Banks County was the only person from home that was with him. He had escorted Wash to several locations in the prison system and had gotten to know him. The sheriff also felt the loss when Wash died.

The Chaplain left the chamber and went to the woodworking shop to see if a casket was there. Even though the prisoners had not gotten to know Wash very well, it was a code among the prisoners to show their respect to him. It was their tribute to Wash as a fellow prisoner. They were working on a casket for his burial when the chaplain came into the shop. The carpenters selected the best and straightest pine boards that were in the shop. It was a simple pine box with square corners and an attached bottom. A removable top capped over the box so it could be nailed shut. They attached rails around the side of boards that were split to be a two by two and used to carry the casket. There were shorter rails attached to the head and foot of the casket as well. They attached the rails to smaller boards on the sides to raise the handrails out enough so that a pallbearer's hand could slide between the rail and casket, making it easier to carry it down the aisle of the church and to the grave.

The prisoners' work on the casket was very precise. They measured each board to the exact length and sawed as straight as possible. When the prisoner finished the casket, they placed pillows in the casket's bottom for the body to rest and an extra pillow for his head. Each person who worked on it carved his name inside the lid. They asked the chaplain what would be a Bible verse to etch on a plaque for the lid, and he told them to put Hebrews 9:27 and John 14:2. They were told the verse did not have to be written out because Wash was familiar with what the verses said. They secured the plaque on the outside of the casket top. They were very careful to make it as neat as they could. They stepped back after they finished. It pleased the prisoners with what they had prepared for Wash Smith.

Chaplain Atkins told the men they should be proud of the work they had completed. After about an hour, they prepared his body for the journey back home. The sheriff had brought Wash's suit during the first trial for him to wear home. He looked at the suit and noticed the necktie was still together as he had tied it for him over two years ago during that first trial. The medical staff dressed Wash in his suit and placed him in the casket. Chaplain Atkins was again with him before the officer from home took him back to Banks County on his last journey. With one last prayer, Atkins gave the white rose to the sheriff. They loaded the casket onto a truck to be taken just outside the prison to a hearse for Wash's last trip home.

It was customary for the prison guards to circle the buildings of the institution before leaving so that prisoners who had gotten to know him could stand at their cell windows and pay their last respect to Wash as he made a last visit to them. The institution was unusually silent for the entire day. Once the truck completed the rounds at the institution, it slowly left the front gate to the awaiting hearse. The body was taken on its cross-country trip back to Banks County.

It took several hours for the sheriff to get Wash's body home from Milledgeville back to his mother. The sheriff grew very weary and refused to leave the casket. It was later in the afternoon when the hearse reached Baldwin. Wash's brother met the hearse at their mother's house and they carried the casket inside. The sheriff gave the picture to his mother and laid the white rose on the casket. The sheriff told his brother he would see him tomorrow at the funeral. They shook hands and departed.

Wash's brother did not go back in the house just then but waited for the hearse to get out of sight down the winding dirt roads toward Baldwin. His brother did not hold any hard feelings toward Sheriff Whelchel. Even though, he was the one who arrested Wash; he was the only one with him from home.

Sheriff Whelchel could not help but think of the last two years and all that Wash had gone through. Even though he knew Wash had committed a crime, he knew that in Wash's mind it was self-defense. The sheriff was thankful that his job was only to arrest and hold, not to try and convict.

***

Sunday, November 23, 1930

Today's funeral will be in the afternoon at Mountain View Baptist Church. Sheriff Whelchel came to the church for the funeral as he told Wash's brother. This time he was not wearing his uniform like all the other times he was around Wash, but he wore a dark suit and tie. As soon as he got there, he went up to Wash's mother

Cordelia, who had not entered the church yet, and told her how sorry he was for her loss. She shook his hand and thanked him for coming. With tears in her eyes, she told Mr. Whelchel how grateful she was for him to have been with her son during his last moments on earth since he was the only person from home to be with him. He stayed outside during the funeral since the church had already filled.

Wash's mother wore black. She had to be helped to the church by her other son, and the funeral service would be very emotional. Tears flowed freely from all that knew Wash. There were no more places in the small white church to sit another person. The room was solemn, with only a sniffle here and there. When the family sat, the funeral began.

EPILOGUE

The story of Wash Smith ends at the church during his burial. He was neither an evil person nor a criminal. Sometimes events in our lives happen. We cannot change once it is over. Many times Wash had wished his life had gone down a different path, but because of that instant, it changed. That instant affected many lives. His life had changed the most. Life was hard for everybody, and you did what you had to do to survive. Wash made a poor choice in his life, but he made good choices too. One choice that he came to realize was that nobody is too bad to become a disciple of Christ. He acknowledged that he had done wrong and was guilty, but he repented. That instant in the store changed his and everybody else's life in the community. The family never talked about it, nor was it a story that would pass to future generations. Almost one hundred years after the event, did anyone know what happened that fateful day in 1928? Trial notes and newspaper articles paved the way for giving one what went on back so many years ago. It gave a visual picture of events. Research into the history of the times helped us see how people lived and how hard life was for people in the Columbia district of Banks County but in Georgia and the nation. A century later, events that happened to Wash, his family, and friends molded their future generations into who they are today. DNA gives us our traits from relatives we never knew. What we receive from DNA, no one can control. A person's eye color, how tall, or types of hair are from the genes that put people together. Word of mouth taught by a person's parents or grandparents passed the tradition down. A person can assume that both DNA and traditions are from a set of people we know or knew. As time passes, one only suspects things they find out that many years ago maybe truer than anybody could imagine. A person can just about know that it passed family traditions down and where they came from. One may only discover the traits from DNA decades later.

The generation discovered these hidden facts fifty years ago and is just now putting together their story over ninety years later. Their struggles and hardships are who we are today. Wash, Sue, Jud, and their relatives created a generation they would be proud. Their part in history ended during the roaring twenties and before the depression. Many of their offspring have made it through to the twenty-first century. Their story is just as intriguing.

Made in the USA
Monee, IL
26 July 2022

4b7d85f5-1025-482d-bba1-7917ac3f12ccR02